TROUBLE WITH VERBS?

Guided discovery materials, exercises and teaching tips at elementary and intermediate levels

David Bolton and Noel Goodey

DELTA PUBLISHING

Trouble With Verbs? contains guided discovery materials and exercises for elementary and intermediate students, together with teaching tips. The book deals with common difficulties that students have with English tenses and verb forms, helping them to make the correct choice when faced with two or more alternatives. It is particularly useful for remedial work.

HOW TO USE THE BOOK

Each of the 15 units can be approached in the following way:

STAGE 1

WHAT'S THE RULE?

 DESIGNED TO PHOTOCOPY

Here, students work on their own.

With the help of pictures and leading questions, **they can work out for themselves** the use of the rule. The *Remember!* box is a reminder of what they have discovered.

They can keep this page in a **personal revision file** for future reference.

STAGE 2

TEACHING POINTS

Students can now work together with you. The material on this page enables you to re-present the rule and tackle the problem in different ways. Of course, you can add your own ideas as well, using immediate contexts or personalised situations.

The *Problem* box lists for you **students' typical mistakes and misunderstandings**.

If necessary, once the TEACHING POINTS have been dealt with, students can go back over the sections in WHAT'S THE RULE? and finish with a final reading of the *Remember!* box.

STAGE 3

CLASSROOM ACTIVITIES

This page offers you a choice of classroom activities and games where students, often working together in pairs or groups, apply the rule in a number of different contexts. They are often invited to use the rule **to talk about themselves and their own lives**.

STAGE 4

PRACTICE EXERCISES

 DESIGNED TO PHOTOCOPY

Here, students work on their own and do the written exercises to check again that they have understood the rule. The exercises are varied and fully contextualised. They provide **a useful objective means of assessing students' understanding**. They can be done in class or at home.

Once you have checked their answers, students can keep this page in their personal file.

NOTES

- Although we recommend the above progression, it is possible to begin a unit with TEACHING POINTS (Stage 2) and to use Stage 1 as a follow-up to your initial presentation.

- If you prefer, students can do Stage 4 before Stage 3.

- In TEACHING POINTS and CLASSROOM ACTIVITIES the class often needs to see a list of sentences. We have kept the lists as short as possible, but, to avoid having to write several sentences on the board, you may prefer to prepare an OHP presentation.

- In TEACHING POINTS, the heading *Extension* introduces a supplementary point concerning the rule. If you feel that, with a particular class, some *Extensions* would be unnecessarily difficult, then you need not present them.

- You can study the units in any order you like. You do not need to work from Unit 1 through to Unit 15. This book enables you to work on key grammar trouble spots **as they arise**.

Present simple OR present continuous?

It rains a lot in England. Look! It's raining.

A Look at the picture.
Put a tick (✔) after sentence 1 or 2.

1 Anna's speaking Spanish. ☐
2 Anna speaks Spanish. ☐

Look at this picture. Put a tick after the correct sentences, 1, 2, 3 or 4.

Excuse me...

1 She's speaking English. ☐
2 She doesn't speak Spanish. ☐
3 She speaks Spanish and English. ☐
4 She isn't speaking Spanish. ☐

Match these sentences with their explanations.

1 She's speaking English. ☐   **a** An action or activity that is in progress now.
2 She speaks English. ☐   **b** A habit, a regular, repeated action or activity.

B Match these two sentences with their explanations.

1 She's learning English at a school in London. ☐   **a** A fact that is always true.
2 All Spanish students learn English at school. ☐   **b** An action or activity happening around now, but probably not at this moment.

C Now look at these sentences.

1 She lives with her parents in Madrid.
2 She's living with an English family in London.

In which sentence are we talking about a temporary situation? ☐
In which sentence is the situation more permanent? ☐

REMEMBER!

Match the six sentences with the explanations. Write present *simple* or *continuous* after each explanation.

1 *Millions of people all over the world speak English.* ☐
2 *Anna goes to English lessons twice a week.* ☐
3 *She's asking the policeman the way to Waterloo station.* ☐
4 *She's going out with an English boy.* ☐
5 *Her parents live in a flat in the north of Madrid.* ☐
6 *She's living in London.* ☐

a An action or activity in progress now.   ▶ Present ....
b A habit, a repeated action.   ▶ Present ....
c A fact that is always true.   ▶ Present ....
d A temporary situation.   ▶ Present ....
e A more permanent situation.   ▶ Present ....
f An action or activity happening around now, but probably not at this moment.   ▶ Present ....

Present simple OR present continuous?

It rains a lot in England. Look! It's raining.

The problem: There are two present tenses in English. Many students find this confusing.

Typical mistakes: *Oh no, it ~~rains~~!*

What ~~do~~ you ~~watch~~? Is it a good film?

I'~~m having~~ a shower every day.

~~Are~~ you ~~understanding~~ me?

- **Temporary or permanent?** Ask students: *What language am I speaking now?*

  Get students to answer: *You're speaking English.*

  Ask students: *What language do I normally speak?*

  Students answer: *You speak (Spanish/Greek/Italian,* etc. = your language)

  Write these two sentences on the board:

  1 *I'm speaking English.*   **2** *I speak (Spanish/Greek/Italian,* etc. = your language)

  Get students to explain the difference:

  1 = Present continuous for a temporary situation.

  2 = Present simple for a more permanent situation.

- **Present action, repeated action or fact?** Write these sentences on the board:

  1 *Steve's playing football.*   **2** *Steve plays football.*   **3** *People all over the world play football.*

  Ask students to explain the difference in meaning:

  1 = Present continuous for action in progress <u>now</u>.

  2 = Present simple for habits or repeated actions (*every day, twice a week*, etc.).

  3 = A fact that is always true.

- **Present continuous for 'now' and 'around now'** Now write these sentences on the board:

  1 *Zoe's having a guitar lesson.*   **2** *Zoe's having guitar lessons.*

  Ask: *In Sentence 1 is Zoe having a guitar lesson now? (Yes.)*

   In Sentence 2 is Zoe having a guitar lesson now? (Possibly, but probably not <u>now</u>.)

  Get students to explain that **1** = an activity happening <u>now</u>, at this moment.

   2 = an activity happening around now, but probably not at this moment.

  Add these examples: **1** *You're learning English now.*

   2 *You're also learning maths and history,* etc.

Extension

- **Present continuous not used with stative verbs** Write these sentences on the board:

  1 *Mmm! I like this spaghetti.*   **2** *I like Italian food.*

  Ask students if these sentences are correct. If they say that sentence 1 is wrong because he's talking about the spaghetti he's eating <u>now</u>, explain to them or remind them that we don't use the present continuous with these common verbs (which describe a state, not an action): *agree, be, believe, belong, contain, exist, forget, hate, have (possession), hear, know, like, love, mean, mind, need, notice, prefer, realise, remember, seem, suppose, understand, want, wish*

Answers to WHAT'S THE RULE? **1:**
A 2; 1,3,4 are correct; 1a 2b   **B** 1b 2a   **C** 2 = temporary 1 = more permanent
REMEMBER! 1c *simple* 2b *simple* 3a *continuous* 4f *continuous* 5e *simple* 6d *continuous*

Present simple OR present continuous?

It rains a lot in England. Look! It's raining.

● **Who is it?**

Every student writes his/her name on a piece of paper, folds it up and puts it in a pile.

Each student takes a piece of paper and writes sentences about the person whose name is on the paper.

Tell students they must write at least two sentences in the present simple and two in the present continuous.

Examples:
She's wearing a black sweater.
She's sitting near the window.

She smiles and laughs a lot.
And she talks a lot.

Students work in groups and take it in turns to read out their sentences. The rest of the group guess who the person is.

● **True or false?**

Read out a list of true and false statements to the class <u>very quickly</u>.

Students write *True* or *False* after they hear each one.

Examples:
1 *I'm speaking English.*
2 *I don't speak (Spanish/Greek/Italian,* etc. = your language)
3 *I teach English.*
4 *I'm teaching English.*
5 *I don't wear glasses.*
6 *I'm not wearing glasses.*
7 *It's raining.*
8 *It rains a lot in the winter.*

● **Correct the mistakes**

Write on the board some sentences that contain common mistakes. Then write the four uses **a** – **d**. Ask students to correct the sentences and match them with their meaning.

Examples:
1 *Be quick! I wait for you.*
2 *Why do you run? We aren't late.*
3 *I'm going on holiday twice a year.*
4 *Oh no! It rains.*
5 *The sun is rising in the east.*
6 *He writes a book about the war.*

a An action happening at this moment.
b A repeated regular action.
c A fact that is always true.
d An activity happening around now, but probably not at this moment.

Answers:
1 a *I'm waiting for you.*
2 a *Why are you running?*
3 b *I go on holiday twice a year.*
4 a *Oh no! It's raining.*
5 c *The sun rises in the east.*
6 d *He's writing a book about the war.*

Answers to PRACTICE EXERCISES 1:
1 1c 2b 3d 4a **2** 1a <u>drives</u> b <u>works</u> c <u>isn't working</u> d <u>is reading</u>; 2a <u>teaches</u> b <u>isn't teaching</u> c <u>is having</u> d <u>is learning</u> e <u>goes</u> **3** 1d 2h 3a 4g 5e 6b 7c 8f **4** 1 *works* 2 *doesn't live* 3 *gets up* 4 *goes* 5 *takes* 6 *doesn't get* 7 *watches* 8 *goes* 9 *has* OR *has got* 10 *works* 11 *isn't working* 12 *'s (is) having* 13 *'s (is) staying* 14 *'s (is) meeting* 15 *'s (is) learning* 16 *'s (is) eating* 17 *enjoys* 18 *'s (is) enjoying* 19 *doesn't want*

Present simple OR present continuous?

It rains a lot in England. Look! It's raining.

1 **Match the sentences with the explanations.**

1 Many people die from smoking. [c]
2 My brother smokes 20 cigarettes a day. [ ]
3 All the family are trying to stop him smoking. [ ]
4 He's smoking a cigarette in bed now! [ ]

a An action or activity in progress now.
b A habit or a repeated action.
c A fact that is always true.
d An action or activity happening around now, but probably not at this moment.

2 **Look at the pictures and underline the correct form of the verb.**

1 a Peter *(drives / is driving)* a taxi in London.
  b He *(works / is working)* 12 hours a day.
  c He *(isn't working / doesn't work)* now.
  d He *(is reading / reads)* a newspaper.

2 a Kate's a teacher. She *(teaches / is teaching)* physics.
  b She *(isn't teaching / doesn't teach)* now.
  c She *(has / is having)* a coffee.
  d She *(learns / is learning)* Greek because ...
  e ... she *(is going / goes)* to Greece every summer.

3 **Match the questions and answers.**

1 What do you do? [d]
2 Are you at university? [ ]
3 What are you studying? [ ]
4 Do you live at home? [ ]
5 Where are you living? [ ]
6 Who are you living with? [ ]
7 Are they studying mathematics too? [ ]
8 Do you go out a lot? [ ]

a Mathematics.
b Two other students.
c No, they aren't.
d I'm a student.
e In a flat, near the university.
f Yes, we do – every night.
g No, I don't.
h Yes, I am.

4 **James is on holiday in Italy. Put the verbs in the present simple or present continuous.**

James (1 work) ...*works*...... in London, but he (2 not live) .... there. Every morning he

(3 get up) .... at 6.00 and he (4 go) .... by train to London. The journey

(5 take) .... an hour and he (6 not get) .... home till 8.00 in the evening.

Then he (7 watch) .... TV and (8 go) .... to bed. He (9 have) ....

a good job, but he (10 work) .... very hard.

He (11 not work) .... now. He (12 have) .... a holiday. He (13 stay) ....

in a hotel in Rimini. He (14 meet) .... a lot of interesting people. He (15 learn) ....

some Italian and he (16 eat) .... a lot of good Italian food.

James (17 enjoy) .... his job, but he (18 enjoy) .... his holiday so much that he

(19 not want) .... to go back to work next week.

Past simple OR present perfect?

I talked to Jack yesterday. He has lost his job.

A Look at the pictures.

Helen's at the station.

Joe's late for work.

Who's speaking? Write *Helen* or *Joe*.

1 ....: *I missed* my train.   (Past simple)

2 ....: *I've missed* my train.   (Present perfect)

B Helen lives in Madrid. She went to live in Spain a year ago.

Joe lives in London. He spent a year in Spain when he was a student.

Who's speaking? Write *Helen* or *Joe*.

1 ....: *I lived* in Spain for a year.   (Past simple)

2 ....: *I've lived* in Spain for a year.   (Present perfect)

C Helen travels a lot.

Put a tick (✔) after the correct question, 1 or 2.

1 Which countries *did you visit*?   (Past simple)   ☐

2 Which countries *have you visited*?   (Present perfect) ☐

D Helen has visited Japan.

Look at Helen's answer and put a tick (✔) after the correct question, 1 or 2.

YOU: **1** When have you visited Japan? ☐   **2** When did you visit Japan? ☐

HELEN: I went there in 1997.

REMEMBER!

Complete these rules. Write *PP (present perfect)* or *PS (past simple)*.
Choose an example sentence from this page for each rule.

1 We use the .... to talk about actions or situations which started in the past, and which continue in the present.

Example: ....

2 We use the .... to talk about an action or a situation that started and finished in the past. We normally say (or understand) exactly when it happened.

Example: ....

3 We use the .... to talk about an action that happened in the past, but we're more interested in the <u>present</u> result of the action.

Example: ....

4 We use the .... to talk about people's experiences, but not when they happened.

Example: ....

Past simple OR present perfect?

I talked to Jack yesterday. He has lost his job.

The problem:	Many students find it difficult to understand that the past simple refers only to the past, whereas the present perfect includes both the past and the present.
Typical mistakes:	*I can't read this note. I ~~lost~~ my glasses.*
	I ~~didn't see~~ this film before.
	I'~~ve finished~~ the book yesterday.
	What ~~have~~ you ~~done~~ last weekend?

● **Past simple or present perfect?** Mime having lost something yourself. Search in your pockets, in your bag, etc.

Get students to say: *What have you lost?* OR *Have you lost something?*
OR *Have you lost your keys/glasses/pen, etc.?*

Tell them what you've lost *(I've lost my keys.)*.

Then find your keys under your books. Hold them up and say:
I've found them! I put my books on top of them.

Write the two sentences on the board: *I've found my keys. I put my books on top of them.*

Ask the students to name the tense in each sentence.

● **Practise the difference** Get individual students to mime the present results of a past action.
Other students say what has happened:
You've eaten too much. You've broken your leg. etc.

Then students ask their classmate further questions, using the past simple:
What did you eat last night? (I ate ...) When did you break your leg? (I broke it ...)

● **Checking students' understanding** Write these two sentences on the board:
1 *My father taught for ten years.* **2** *My father has taught for ten years.*

Indicate sentence 1 and ask the class: *Is my father a teacher now?*

Indicate sentence 2. Ask the same question.

Then write: **1** *I stayed with an English family last year.*
2 *I've stayed with an English family last year.*

Ask students to say which sentence is wrong and to explain why.

NOTE: British English/American English
In American English the past simple is often used where, in British English, the present perfect is used.
For example:

British English	American English
I've just seen him.	▶ *I just saw him.*
I've already finished.	▶ *I already finished.*
Have you ever ridden a motorbike?	▶ *Did you ever ride a motorbike?*

Answers to WHAT'S THE RULE? 2:
A 1 *Joe* 2 *Helen*   **B** 1 *Joe* 2 *Helen*   **C** 2✔   **D** 2✔
REMEMBER! 1 *PP: I've lived in Spain for a year.* 2 *PS: I missed my train.* OR *I lived in Spain for a year.* OR *Which countries did you visit?*
OR *When did you go to Japan?* OR *I went there in 1997.* 3 *PP: I've missed my train.* 4 *PP: Which countries have you visited?*

9

Past simple or present perfect?

I talked to Jack yesterday. He has lost his job.

● **What did you do? What have you done?**

Ask students to say or write:

a two or three things **they did** last week.
I bought some new shoes last week.

b two or three things **they've done** this week.
I've washed my hair three times.

AND/OR

Get students to write sentences about the things they've done this week, using these verbs: *buy read break go see lose*

Example:
I've bought a Bob Marley CD. I bought it on Monday.

● **Have you ever ...?**

Get students to work in pairs and ask each other questions with: *Have you ever ...?*

Then they add extra questions, using the past simple:
When did you ...?
Did you enjoy ...?
Why did you ...? etc.

Examples:
(eat) Chinese food
> **Have you ever eaten** *Chinese food?*
> **When did you eat** *Chinese food?*

(have) an operation
(break) an arm
(fly) across the Atlantic
(meet) an English person

● **Who's done what?**

Individual students ask questions to find out which members of the class have ...

... flown in a plane
... been in a balloon
... been to England
... ridden a motorbike
... seen a ghost
... done a bungee jump
... been to the USA
... been on TV
... met a famous person

Then ask additional questions in the past simple.

Example:
(*Who has flown in a plane?*
I have.)

*When **did** you **fly** in a plane?*
When I went to London.

*When **did** you **go** to London?*
I went last year.

● **Write sentences**

Get students to write two sentences with the present perfect and two sentences with the past simple. Each sentence must show that the particular tense is essential.

Examples:
*Look! It **has started** to rain.*
***Have** you **seen** any good films recently?*

*I **didn't sleep** well last night.*
*I **got up** late this morning.*

Answers to PRACTICE EXERCISES 2:
1 1a 2b   **2** 1 have you been 2 did 3 was 4 have been 5 Have you travelled 6 have been 7 went 8 Have you visited
9 haven't 10 Have you made 11 have made 12 bought   **3** 1c 2f 3a 4b 5d 6e
4 1 ~~has built~~ built 2✔ 3 ~~lived~~ has lived OR have lived 4 ~~has decided~~ decided 5 ~~visited~~ have visited
5 1 I've lived in Milan for ten years. 2 I started studying English five years ago. 3 I've been at university for two years.
4 I met my girlfriend Gemma a year ago. 5 She's lived in Italy for three years. 6 We bought a car last week.

Past simple OR present perfect?

I talked to Jack yesterday. He has lost his job.

1 **Look at these two sentences.**

    1 Jack has broken his leg. ☐   **2** Jack broke his leg. ☐

    Which of these sentences follow 1 and 2? Write *a* or *b* in the boxes.

    a He can't walk.   **b** He was in hospital for two days.

2 <u>Underline</u> **the correct verb form.**

    NIC: How long (1) <u>*have you been*</u> / *were you* a model?

    TARA: I (2) *have done* / *did* my first job when I (3) *was* / *have been* 16, so I (4) *was* / *have been* a model for two years.

    NIC: (5) *Have you travelled* / *Did you travel* a lot?

    TARA: Yes. I (6) *went* / *have been* to a lot of interesting places. Last month I (7) *have been* / *went* to Thailand.

    NIC: (8) *Have you visited* / *Did you visit* the USA?

    TARA: No, I (9) *didn't* / *haven't*.

    NIC: (10) *Have you made* / *Did you make* much money?

    TARA: Yes, I (11) *made* / *have made* a lot. Last year I (12) *have bought* / *bought* a sports car and a villa in Ibiza!

3 **Match the two halves of each sentence.**

1 Kelly can't go to school …	c	**a**	for five days now.
2 She broke it …	☐	**b**	before.
3 She's been in hospital …	☐	**c**	because she's broken her arm.
4 She's never been in hospital …	☐	**d**	and she's brought her some fruit.
5 Her friend Zoe has come to see her, …	☐	**e**	and she brought her some magazines.
6 Zoe came to see her yesterday ….	☐	**f**	in a road accident last week.

4 **Look at the verb forms in these sentences about Buckingham Palace. If the verb form is wrong,** ~~cross it out~~ **and write the correct form. If the verb form is correct, put a tick (✔).**

    1 The Duke of Buckingham ~~has built~~ the palace in 1703.   …………*built*…………

    2 King George III bought it in 1761.   ……………………………

    3 The Royal Family lived in the palace since 1837.   ……………………………

    4 In 1995 Queen Elizabeth has decided to open the palace to the public.   ……………………………

    5 Since 1995 thousands of tourists visited the palace.   ……………………………

5 **Luigi is an Italian student. Complete the sentences.**

    1 I came to live in Milan ten years ago. I (live) ……*'ve lived*…… in Milan for ……*ten years*…… .

    2 I've studied English for five years. I (start) ……*started*…… studying English five years ……*ago*…… .

    3 I started university two years ago. I (be) ………………… at university for ………………… .

    4 I've known my English girlfriend Gemma for a year. I (meet) ………………… my girlfriend Gemma a year ………………… .

    5 She came to live in Italy three years ago. She (live) ………………… in Italy ………………… three years.

    6 We've bought a car – an old Fiat. We (buy) ………………… a car last week.

🐱 *DESIGNED TO PHOTOCOPY*

Present perfect simple OR present perfect continuous?

Helen has played three games of tennis. Sam has been playing football – he's tired.

A Look at the pictures. Match the sentences with the pictures.

1 ☐   **2** ☐

a James has painted his bedroom.

b James has been painting his bedroom.

Now match the sentences with these explanations:

1 An action which has continued until now. It may be finished or unfinished.   ☐

2 A completed or finished action.   ☐

B Look at these sentences.

   a He's been painting for two hours.   (Present perfect continuous)

   b He's painted two walls.   (Present perfect simple)

   c He's painted one wall three times.   (Present perfect simple)

Complete these rules. Write *PPS (present perfect simple)* or *PPC (present perfect continuous)*.

1 We must use the .... when we talk about the number of things someone has done.

2 We must use the .... when we talk about the number of times someone has done something.

Now answer this question, *Yes* or *No*.

3 Can we say *He's been painting* one wall three times?   ....

```
┌─ REMEMBER! ─────────────────────────────────────────────────────────────┐
```

Complete these rules. Write *PPS (present perfect simple)* or *PPC (present perfect continuous)*.
Choose an example sentence from this page for each rule.

1 We use the .... when we talk about a completed or finished action.

   Example: ....

2 We use the .... when we talk about <u>how many</u> times or <u>how many</u> things.

   Example: ....

3 We use the .... when it's important to say that an action or situation has been
<u>continuous</u> over a period of time until now.

   Example: ....

Present perfect simple OR present perfect continuous?

Helen has played three games of tennis. Sam has been playing football – he's tired.

The problem: Many students use the present perfect simple where they should use the present perfect continuous, and vice versa.

Typical mistakes: *Your eyes are red. ~~Have~~ you ~~cried~~? I've ~~been phoning~~ her five times. I've ~~been knowing~~ her for a long time.*

● **Use of present perfect simple and continuous** Hold up a book and write these two sentences on the board: **1** *I've been reading this book.* **2** *I've read this book.*

Ask students: *In sentence 1, do you know if I've finished the book or not?*
Help students to see that they can't be sure.

Then ask: *So, in sentence 1 which is more important – if I've finished the book or not OR the action (my reading) that has continued over a period of time?*
Help students to understand that the action (your reading) is more important.

Now ask: *In sentence 2, which is more important – the activity of reading the book OR the fact that you've finished the book? (The fact that you've finished the book.)*

Finally, ask students to explain the difference between the two sentences:
1 *I've been reading this book.* (Present perfect continuous for an action which has continued until now and may continue in the future.)
2 *I've read this book.* (Present perfect simple for a completed action. We don't say <u>when</u> it happened.)

Explain again that in sentence 1 it isn't important whether you've finished the book or not. The important thing is that the action has continued over a period of time.

● **Present perfect simple with 'how many'** Write this sentence on the board:
I've been reading this book.

Get students to ask you a question starting *How long ...*
(How long have you been reading it?) Answer their question: *I've been reading it for (two weeks).*

Get students to ask you a question starting *How many pages ...*
(How many pages have you read?) Answer: *I've read (150) pages.*

Get students to ask you a question starting *How many books ...*
(How many books has this author written?) Answer: *She's written (three).*

Extension
● **Present perfect continuous not used with stative verbs** Remind students or explain that the following verbs are not usually used in the continuous form:
agree, be, believe, belong, contain, exist, forget, hate, have (possession), hear, know, like, love, mean, mind, need, notice, prefer, realise, remember, seem, suppose, understand, want, wish

Check their understanding by writing up these sentences and asking which form of the verb is correct:
1 James (*has had/has been having*) his flat for two months.
2 He (*has hated/has been hating*) the colour of his bedroom for a long time.

Answers to WHAT'S THE RULE? 3:
A 1a 2b; 1b 2a   **B** 1 *PPS* 2 *PPS* 3 *No*
REMEMBER! 1 *PPS: James has painted his bedroom.* 2 *PPS: He's painted two walls./He's painted one wall three times.*
3 *PPC: James/He's been painting his bedroom/for two hours.*

Present perfect simple or present perfect continuous?

Helen has played three games of tennis. Sam has been playing football – he's tired.

● **Who's lying?**

a Students form groups of three. Each member of the group should write two sentences, one in the present perfect simple, the other in the present perfect continuous. Two students should write true sentences, one student should write sentences which are <u>not</u> true.

b Each group should read out their sentences. The rest of the class guess who the liar is.

Examples:

A: *I've passed my driving test.*
I've been living in this town for 12 years.

B: *I've broken both my legs.*
I've been going out with the same girl for over a year.

C: *I've been to New York.*
(<u>not</u> true)
I've been learning to ski.
(<u>not</u> true)

C is the liar.

● **What's been happening?**

Students work in pairs. Together they write two sentences in the present perfect simple and two in the present perfect continuous about what <u>has happened</u> and what <u>has been happening</u> in their school/area/city/country recently.

Examples:
Our football team has won three matches!
They've been playing very well.
A new electronics factory has opened.
It's been raining since the weekend.

● **What's the news?**

Work in groups. Each group should choose one of the following news stories:

Hollywood star to marry man 20 years younger
Train crash: over 50 killed
Princess leaves hospital after operation
Pop singer has baby
Murder of 93-year-old woman: man arrested
5 men escape from prison

Each group writes the complete news story, using at least two examples of the present perfect simple and two of the present perfect continuous.

Example:

Hollywood star to marry man 20 years younger
He has been working as her hairdresser for the last two years.
They have been going out together for six months.
She has had four husbands.
They have invited 1500 guests to the wedding.

Answers to PRACTICE EXERCISES 3:
1 1 a 2 c 3 a 4 b 5 c 6 b   **2** 1 *Joe has been cooking. He's made two pizzas. He's eaten one of them.* 2 *Joanna's (has) been painting her room. She's painted two walls. She's decided she doesn't like the colour.* 3 *Tessa's (has) been working hard. She's had ten cups of coffee. She's finished work now.* 4 *Jake's (has) been using the phone. He's been talking for an hour. He's phoned four friends.* 5 *Nick and Rachel have been cleaning the house. They've (have) been working since 2 o'clock. They haven't finished yet.*
3 1 <u>What have you been doing?</u> 2 <u>I've been working</u> 3 <u>I've been working</u> 4 <u>I've been trying</u> 5 <u>I've been doing</u> 6 <u>I've done</u> 7 <u>I've been trying</u> 8 <u>I've tried</u> 9 <u>hasn't answered</u>

Present perfect simple OR present perfect continuous?

Helen has played three games of tennis. Sam has been playing football – he's tired.

1 **Match the sentences 1 – 6 with the explanations a, b and c.**

1 A plane has crashed in Scotland. [a]

2 Helicopters have been searching the area. ☐

3 They have now found the crashed plane. ☐

4 Ambulances have tried two or three times to reach it. ☐

5 But it's been snowing all day. ☐

6 And the snow has blocked two mountain roads. ☐

a A completed or finished action.

b A statement giving information about <u>how many</u> times or <u>how many</u> things.

c A sentence where it's important to say that an action or situation has been <u>continuous</u> over a period of time until now.

2 **Six students are living together in the same house. It's 6 o'clock on Saturday evening. Complete these sentences. Use the present perfect simple and the present perfect continuous.**

1 Joe / cook   *Joe has been cooking.*

   He / make / two pizzas   *He's made two pizzas.*

   He / eat / one of them   *He's eaten one of them.*

2 Joanna / paint / her room   ....

   She / painted / two walls   ....

   She / decide / she doesn't like the colour   ....

3 Tessa / work hard   ....

   She / have / ten cups of coffee   ....

   She / finish / work now   ....

4 Jake / use / the phone   ....

   He / talk / for an hour   ....

   He / phone / four friends   ....

5 Nick and Rachel / clean / the house   ....

   They / work / since 2 o' clock   ....

   They / not finish / yet   ....

3 <u>Underline</u> **the better alternative.**

A: You look tired. (1) <u>*What have you been doing*</u> / *What have you done?*

B: I'm very tired. (2) *I've worked* / *I've been working* for four hours. In fact, (3) *I've been working* / *I've worked* since 6 o'clock. (4) *I've tried* / *I've been trying* to do my maths homework. (5) *I've been doing* / *I've done* it all evening. There are twelve questions and (6) *I've done* / *I've been doing* eleven, but I can't do the last one. Anna's very good at maths. (7) *I've been trying* / *I've tried* to phone her all evening. (8) *I've tried* / *I've been trying* five times but she (9) *hasn't answered* / *hasn't been answering* the phone yet.

Past simple OR past continuous?

I went to the beach. The sun was shining. When I arrived, my friends were swimming.

A Look at the picture. Match sentences 1 and 2 with a and b.

1 Harry *had* breakfast at 7.30.　　(Past simple) ☐

2 Harry *was having* breakfast at 7.30.　(Past continuous) ☐

a He started breakfast <u>before</u> 7.30.
b He started breakfast <u>at</u> 7.30.

Which sentence, 1 or 2, describes the picture? ☐

B Look at the picture. Match the questions and answers.

1 What *did* he *do* when he *heard* the news? ☐

2 What *was* he *doing* when he *heard* the news? ☐

a He *was having* breakfast when he *heard* the news.
b He *dropped* his cup when he *heard* the news!

Match answers a and b with these explanations:

1 A short action in the middle of a longer action. ☐

2 Two past actions that followed, one <u>after</u> the other. ☐

C Read the following:

Harry *went* out. It *was raining*. People *were carrying* umbrellas. He *took* the 8.00 bus into town. Everyone *was talking* about the President.

Which sentences are a general description of the scene or situation? Tick (✔) sentences 1 or 2.

1 He went out. He took the 8.00 bus into town. ☐

2 It was raining. People were carrying umbrellas. Everyone was talking about the President. ☐

D Now look at these sentences.

Harry was a teacher. (1) He *lived* in an apartment in Boston.
But his mother was ill, so (2) he *was living* with her for a few weeks.

In which sentence, 1 or 2, is the situation temporary, only for a short time? ☐

In which sentence is the situation more permanent, more normal? ☐

REMEMBER!

Complete these rules. Write *PS (past simple)* or *PC (past continuous)*.
Choose an example sentence from this page for each rule.

1 We use the .... to talk about an action that started before a particular time in the past and was still in progress at that particular time.

Example: ....

2 We use the .... to describe a scene in the past – continuing, unfinished actions.

Example: ....

3 We use the .... to talk about completed actions in the past.

Example: ....

4 We use the .... to talk about a temporary situation in the past.

Example: ....

5 We use the .... to talk about past situations that were permanent, not temporary.

Example: ....

Past simple OR past continuous?

I went to the beach. The sun was shining. When I arrived, my friends were swimming.

The problem: Students use the past simple where they should use the past continuous, and vice versa.

Typical mistakes: *I ~~had~~ a bath when the phone rang.   I ~~was playing~~ tennis a lot when I was young. My sister ~~was liking~~ maths when she was at school.*

● **Action in progress or completed?** Write these two sentences on the board:
8.00: Helen left home.   8.30: She arrived at school.
Ask: *What did she do at 8.00? What did she do at 8.30?* **What was she doing at 8.15?**
Write the answer on the board: *At 8.15 she was going to school.* (Past continuous)

● **Two past actions in same sentence** Write these two sentences on the board:
1 *We were having dinner when John arrived.*   **2** *We had dinner when John arrived.*
Ask: *In sentence 1, when did they start having dinner? (Before John arrived)*
Now ask: *In sentence 2, were they having dinner before John arrived? (No.)*
Draw two time lines, 1 and 2:

1 xxxxxxxxxxxxxxxxxxxxxxxxxxxxxxxxxxxx   **2** ....|...................|...................
.......................|.....................................   John arrived   xxxxxxxxxx
                    John arrived

Ask students to replace xxxxx with *We **had** dinner* OR *We **were having** dinner*

● **Past continuous for general description** Describe what was happening when you left home this morning: *The sun was shining but a cold wind was blowing. A lot of people were hurrying to catch the bus. I was feeling tired.*
Ask: *What tense did I use in my description? (The past continuous.)*
Ask: *Why did I use this tense? (Because you were giving a general description of the situation at the time.)*

● **Permanent or temporary?** Write these two sentences on the board:
1 *Jack worked in a restaurant.*   **2** *Jack was working in a restaurant.*
Ask students to match sentences 1 and 2 with **a** or **b**: **a** *He was a waiter.* **b** *He was a student.*

Then ask students to suggest possible reasons for sentence 2.
He wasn't going to stay there very long. It wasn't a permanent job. etc.

Extension

● **Further uses of the past simple** We normally use the past simple (not the past continuous) for:
Past habits: *When I was young, I **watched** TV a lot.* (NOT I ~~was watching~~)
(Here the past simple has the meaning of *used to. – I used to watch TV a lot.*)
Repeated past actions: *We **danced** together five times.* (NOT We ~~were dancing~~)

● **Past continuous not used with stative verbs** Remind students or explain that the following verbs are not usually used in the continuous form:
agree, be, believe, belong, contain, exist, forget, hate, have (possession), hear, know, like, love, mean, mind, need, notice, prefer, realise, remember, seem, suppose, understand, want, wish

---

Answers to WHAT'S THE RULE? 4:
A 1 b 2 a; 2   **B** 1 b 2 a 1 a; 2 b   **C** 2 ✔   **D** 2 temporary, only for a short time 1 more permanent, more normal
REMEMBER! 1 PC *Harry was having breakfast at 7.30.* etc. 2 PC *It was raining.* etc. 3 PS *He went out.* etc. 4 PC *He was living with her for a few weeks.* 5 PS *He lived in an apartment in Boston.*

Past simple OR past continuous?

I went to the beach. The sun was shining. When I arrived, my friends were swimming.

● **Disasters**

Students imagine a disaster – an earthquake, a ship sinking, a coach crash, etc.

Individually they make notes in answer to the questions:

1 *What were you/your friends/your family doing when the ship started to sink?*

2 *What did you/your friends do?*

Students, acting as reporters, go round the class asking others about the disaster.
What were you doing when ...?
Were you watching TV when ...?
What did you do?
Did you run away?
Did you shout for help? etc.

● **Describe your morning**

Students write a short report of what happened and what was happening when they left home this morning.

Example:
I left home at 8.00. The sun was shining. People were going to work. The traffic was moving slowly. I caught the bus at 8.10. I met my friends on the bus. The bus was noisy. Everybody was talking and laughing. I arrived at college at 8.20.

● **What were you doing when ...?**

Students write sentences about something that really happened to them, or about an imaginary past situation. They say what happened when/while they were having a shower/having breakfast/walking by the river/painting their bedroom walls, etc. Write an example on the board:

While I was coming to school this morning, the bus lost a wheel. Everyone was talking normally. Then suddenly we fell out of our seats.

Students then tell their stories to the rest of the class.

● **Game: Alibi**

You describe a murder that took place yesterday evening – the victim, the scene, etc.

One student, (A), is suspected of committing the murder. He/she leaves the room with a second student, (B). Together they create an alibi for A. They must agree where they met, what time they met, what they were wearing, what they did, etc., yesterday evening to prove that at the time of the murder they couldn't possibly have been near the scene of the crime.

Meanwhile the other students in the class prepare questions.

Student A then comes back into the room and answers the questions.

Student B comes back into the room and answers the same questions.

If Students A and B answer the questions in very different ways, then A's alibi is proved to be false and he/she is the murderer.

Examples of questions:
What were you doing at 8.15 yesterday evening?
What were you wearing when you met A/B?
What did you do when you met A/B?

Past simple OR past continuous?

I went to the beach. The sun was shining. When I arrived, my friends were swimming.

1 Match the sentences with the correct explanation.

1 Kate lived in London.   ☐c   a A completed past action.

2 She was staying with a friend in the country.   ☐   b A description of a scene.

3 It was warm and the sun was shining.   ☐   c A permanent past situation.

4 They decided to play tennis.   ☐   d A past action interrupted by another.

5 While they were playing, it started to rain.   ☐   e A temporary past situation.

2 Last night there was a storm and all the lights went out in Kate's house.
Complete the sentences, then put them in the right column.

Kate (1 read) .... a book. Her mother (2 look) .... for some candles.

Her sisters (3 watch) .... TV. Her grandmother (4 fall) .... downstairs.

Her brother (5 listen) .... to his stereo. Her father (6 phone) .... the

electricity company.

1 What were Kate's family doing when the lights went out?	2 What did Kate's family do when the lights went out?
Kate was reading a book.	*Her mother looked for some candles.*
....	....
....	....

3 Put the verbs in the past simple or the past continuous.

Yesterday Carlos (1 get up) .....*got up*........ early and (2 have) .... breakfast.

He (3 leave) .... the house at 8.00 and (4 arrive) .... at school at 8.30.

Carlos (5 study) .... English at a school in London. He (6 stay) .... with an English

family in Kensington. He (7 be) .... from Mexico. He (8 live) .... in Veracruz.

He (9 learn) .... English because he (10 want) .... to work in the USA.

When he (11 arrive) .... at school, his Italian friend, Claudia, (12 wait) .... for him.

They (13 have) .... a cup of coffee before their first class.

4 Look at the verb forms in this story. If the verb form is correct, put a tick (✔).
If the verb form is wrong, ~~cross it out~~ and write the correct form.

I ~~was going~~ to a club last night and I saw a good-looking boy. When   1 ...*went*...............

I arrived at the club people talked to each other, but nobody was   2 ....

dancing because the music wasn't very good. I was having a drink,   3 ....

then I decided to go home. I looked for my bag when someone asked   4 ....

me to dance. It was the good-looking boy! He was wearing a   5 ....

red shirt and black boots. When he was asking me to dance, I said   6 ....

'yes' immediately. We danced together all evening. I realised that   7 ....

everyone in the club watched us. At the end of the evening we were   8 ....

having a drink together when suddenly he got up and said goodbye.   9 ....

He wasn't asking for my telephone number, and I never saw him again!   10 ....

🐱 DESIGNED TO PHOTOCOPY

5 | WHAT'S THE RULE?

Past simple OR past perfect?

She walked home because someone had stolen her car. He went out when he had finished his lunch.
When they saw my new hat they laughed.

A Look at the picture and the sentences.

Adam's alarm clock normally wakes him at 7.00.
Yesterday Adam woke up at 7.30.
His alarm clock **had stopped** at 5.20!

```
PAST          5.20              7.30          NOW
.....................|.................|.........................
        His clock stopped.    He woke up.
```

PAST SIMPLE   PAST PERFECT
He **woke up** late because his alarm clock **had stopped** at 5.20.

In this sentence there were two actions at different times in the past:

The first action/event = past perfect. The second action/event = past simple.

Now answer these questions:

1 What happened at 7.30? ....

2 What had happened before that, at 5.20? ....

B Look at the pictures.
Match the sentences
with the pictures.

a He **had brushed** his hair when
he **left** the house.

b He **brushed** his hair when
he **had left** the house.

1 ☐   2 ☐

C Look at the picture and this sentence.

When Adam **looked** at his watch, he **jumped** out of bed.

Now answer these questions, *Yes* or *No*.

1 Did the two actions (*looked* / *jumped*) happen at
nearly the same time? ....

2 Are either of the two verbs in the past perfect? ....

REMEMBER!

Complete these rules, using *PS (past simple)* or *PP (past perfect)*.
Choose an example sentence from this page for each rule.

1 We use the .... to talk about an action or event that happened <u>before</u> another action or event in the past.

Example: ....

2 When two actions in the past happened at nearly the same moment, when one action was an immediate
reaction to another action, we use the .... for both actions.

Example: ....

Past simple OR past perfect?

She walked home because someone had stolen her car. He went out when he had finished his lunch.
When they saw my new hat they laughed.

The problem: Students aren't sure when to use the past perfect when they're talking about two different times/actions in the past.

Typical mistakes: *I went to the police station, but nobody ~~found~~ my bag.*
The classroom was empty. All the students ~~left~~.
He watched TV and ~~had gone~~ to bed.

● **The difference between the past simple and the past perfect** Write these two sentences on the board:
1 *At 7.30 the film started.*   **2** *At 7.30 the film had started.*
Ask: *What time did the film start in sentence 1? (It started at 7.30.)*
Ask: *Did the film also start at 7.30 in sentence 2? (No, it didn't. It started before 7.30.)*
Ask: *What tense is **started**? (The past simple.) What tense is **had started**? (The past perfect.)*

● **Use of the past perfect** Write this sentence on the board:
When he arrived, everybody had left.
Ask: *How many people were there when he arrived?*
    (None. They had all left.)
Ask: *What happened first and what happened <u>after</u> that?*
    (Everybody left first and he arrived after that.)

Now write these two sentences on the board:
1 *Her father had died when she left university.*   **2** *Her father died when she had left university.*
Ask: *In sentence 1, did he die before she left university? (Yes.)*
    In sentence 2, did he die while she was at university? (No.)
Get students to explain the difference.

● **Practise the difference** Mime finishing a meal and then turning on a TV.
Get students to say what happened, starting *When ...*
(Example: When you had finished your dinner, you turned on the TV.)

Get students to mime two consecutive actions. Other students in the class can then say
or write what happened, using *When* + the past perfect + the past simple.
Examples: *When Claudia **had brushed** her hair, she **put** her brush in her bag.*
    *When Maria **had done** her homework, she **phoned** her friend.*

● **Past simple + past simple = action ▶ reaction** Write these sentences on the board:
1 *When she saw him, she smiled.*   **2** *I answered the phone when it rang.*
Explain that each sentence is about two different actions in the past.
Ask: *Which tense are both verbs in?*
    (The past simple.)
Ask: *Why do we use two verbs in the past simple in sentences like these?*
    (Because one action is an immediate reaction to another action.)
Get students to give their own examples of this use of verbs in the past simple where one action is an
immediate reaction to another.

Answers to WHAT'S THE RULE? 5:
A **1** *He woke up.* **2** *His alarm clock had stopped.*   **B** 1b 2a   **C** 1 Yes 2 No   **REMEMBER!** 1 *PP: His alarm clock had stopped.*
OR *He had brushed his hair.* **2** *PS: When Adam looked at his watch, he jumped out of bed.*

Past simple OR past perfect?

She walked home because someone had stolen her car. He went out when he had finished his lunch. When they saw my new hat they laughed.

● **What had you done?**

Students complete these sentences, using the past perfect. They then work in pairs and compare their answers.

Example:
*By 4 o'clock yesterday afternoon I **had arrived home and had had a sandwich**.*
By 7 o'clock yesterday evening I ...
By 9 o'clock last night ...
By 9 o'clock this morning ...

● **A memorable experience**

Students work in pairs. They each think of a past experience that was really important to them:

A trip to another country / A frightening experience / A (birthday) party / My first day at a new school, etc.

Students then write sentences like these, using the past simple and past perfect:
*I **went** to New York last summer. I **hadn't had** a holiday in the USA before and I **had** never **visited** a big city like New York. I **stayed** for two weeks with my uncle in Brooklyn.*

*When I **was** five, I **lost** my mother in the street. I **had** never **lost** her before and I **was** very scared. A policeman **stopped** me. I **had** never **spoken** to a policeman before.*

Students read their sentences to each other. Then one of them tells the rest of the class about his/her partner's experience.

● **Think of a reason**

Students complete these sentences, using a verb in the past perfect:
He was sick three times because ...
He had a hole in his trousers because ...
She cried because ...
She rang the police because ...
He phoned her because ...
They took him to hospital because ...
His face was red because ...
He hit him because ...

Students then work in groups and choose the group's 'best' sentences and read them to the class.

Answers to PRACTICE EXERCISES 5:
1 1 b   2 a   3 c   **2** 1 'd waited; arrived   2 went; had seen   3 wasn't; had already eaten   4 went; hadn't eaten   5 had looked; ordered 6 was; had got up   7 got; had stolen   **3** 1 had got up got up   2 ✔   3 had cycled cycled   4 arranged had arranged   5 left had left 6 ✔   7 had remembered remembered   8 disappeared had disappeared   **4** 1 was   2 lived   3 went   4 had changed   5 visited 6 didn't recognise   7 had painted   8 had cut   9 had built   10 had closed   11 had become   12 met   13 had changed   14 had got   15 had 16 saw   17 hadn't changed   18 hadn't got   19 looked   20 was   21 didn't recognise

Past simple OR past perfect?

She walked home because someone had stolen her car. He went out when he had finished his lunch.
When they saw my new hat they laughed.

1 **Match the sentences with the rules.**

1 When Suzanne had finished her book, she turned on the television. ☐ *b*

2 At 11.30, everyone except Suzanne had gone to bed. ☐

3 When the phone rang at 11.45 she answered it. ☐

a We use the past perfect for an action that happened before a certain time in the past.

b We use the past perfect to talk about an action that happened before another action in the past.

c We use two verbs in the past simple when an action in the past was an immediate reaction to another action.

2 **Underline** **the correct alternative in this description of a terrible evening.**

1 After I (*'d waited* / *waited*) for half an hour, she finally (*had arrived* / *arrived*).

2 We (*had gone* / *went*) to the cinema but she (*had seen* / *saw*) the film before.

3 She (*hadn't been* / *wasn't*) hungry because she (*already ate* / *had already eaten*).

4 But we (*went* / *had gone*) to a restaurant because I (*didn't eat* / *hadn't eaten*).

5 When we (*had looked* / *looked*) at the menu, we (*ordered* / *had ordered*) two pizzas.

6 She (*was* / *had been*) tired because she (*had got up* / *got up*) early.

7 When we (*got* / *had got*) back to my car, I found that someone (*stole* / *had stolen*) the radio.

3 **If the verb form is wrong, ~~cross it out~~ and write the correct form. Put a tick (✔) if the sentence is correct.**

1 Katherine ~~had got up~~ after her parents had gone to work. ....*got up*........

2 After she had had a shower, she made herself some breakfast. ....

3 As soon as she had eaten her breakfast, she had cycled into town. ....

4 She arranged the day before to meet her friends at 10.00. ....

5 But it was 10.15 now and her friends left. ....

6 After she'd waited for a few minutes, she went into a shop. ....

7 Then she had remembered she had forgotten to lock her bike. ....

8 When she came out, her bike disappeared. ....

4 **Put the verbs in the past simple or the past perfect.**

When I (1 be) ..*was*... a boy I (2 live) .... in a town called Melksham.

Last week I (3 go) .... back to Melksham. It (4 change) .... !

First I (5 visit) .... my old house. I (6 not recognise) .... it.

They (7 paint) .... it green, they (8 cut) .... down all the trees in the

garden and they (9 build) .... a garage there instead. And the railway station at the end

of the road (10 close) .... It (11 become) .... a supermarket. In the road,

I (12 meet) .... an old girlfriend. She (13 change) .... completely too.

She (14 get) .... married, and now she (15 have) .... three children!

In the pub I (16 see) .... my old friend Mick. He (17 not change) ....

– he (18 not get) .... married and he still (19 look) .... exactly the same.

There (20 be) .... only one problem – he (21 not recognise) .... me!

🐱 DESIGNED TO PHOTOCOPY

Future: *going to* OR *will* OR present continuous?

My friend is going to live in Italy. That boat is going to sink – there are too many passengers.
Goodbye. I'll see you tomorrow. – I can't see you tomorrow. I'm playing tennis.

A Present continuous

Gill's got a new boyfriend, Jack.
She's looking at her diary.
GILL: *I'm meeting* Jack at 8.30 next Saturday.

1 Has Jack agreed to meet Gill next Saturday? ....

2 Is Gill talking about **a** an arrangement OR **b** a possibility? ☐

B Going to

Gill wants a new dress for Saturday
GILL: *I'm going to buy* a new dress.

Gill has made a decision. What is her plan now?

She ………..................……….. a new dress.

C Going to

Gill wants to go into town to buy her dress.
She's looking at some black clouds.
GILL: I need an umbrella. *It's going to rain.*

1 Is it raining now? ....

2 What seems certain because of the black clouds?

It ………...................…………... rain.

D Will

Gill's phoning Jack about Saturday.
GILL: I'm getting the 7.45 bus.
So, *I'll arrive* in town at 8.15.

The bus into town usually takes 30 minutes.
What time will the 7.45 arrive in town?

It ………..........................…... at 8.15. (This is a simple future fact.)

E Will

GILL: Can you meet me?
JACK: Yes. *I'll meet* you at the bus station.

Does Jack decide to meet Gill **a** before she asks the question

OR **b** at the moment he speaks? ☐

REMEMBER!

Match the sentences with the explanations.

1 *Jack 's seeing* Gill at 8.30 next Saturday. ☐

2 *Gill and Jack* **will be** in town next Saturday evening. ☐

3 *Goodbye, I'll phone you tomorrow.* ☐

4 *I'm going to wear* my new dress on Saturday. ☐

5 *There's a hole in Gill's new dress.*
She looks very unhappy – she's going to cry. ☐

a An intention, a plan made <u>before</u> the moment of speaking.
b An intention, a decision that we make now, at the moment of speaking.
c A simple future fact.
d An arrangement made for a particular time in the future.
e A future event or action that seems certain because of something we can see now.

Future: *going to* OR *will* OR present continuous?

My friend is going to live in Italy. That boat is going to sink – there are too many passengers.
Goodbye. I'll see you tomorrow. – I can't see you tomorrow. I'm playing tennis.

The problem: Students confuse these three different ways of talking about the future.
Typical mistakes: *Don't go to Florida in July. It's going to be too hot.* (It'll be …)
I've just heard the weather forecast. It'll rain. (It's going to …)
Can I speak to Gill? – Yes, I'm going to call her. (I'll call …)
I see Jack next Saturday. (I'm seeing …)
What's Gill's number? I'm phoning her. (I'm going to …)

● **Different uses of *will*/*going to*/present continuous** Write these four sentences on the board
(don't write the explanations in brackets):
1 *I'm seeing the doctor.* (The arrangement has been made some time before.)
2 *I'll see the doctor.* (A decision made now <u>at</u> the moment of speaking.)
3 *I'm going to see the doctor.* (A decision made <u>before</u> the moment of speaking.)
4 *I'll see the doctor.* (A simple future fact.)

Tell students that all four sentences refer to the future.

Help them to put each sentence into a context that explains the use of the present
continuous (1), *will* (2), *going to* (3) and *will* (4).
Examples: 1 *I can't come tomorrow evening. **I'm seeing the doctor** at 6.30.*
2 *Your arm might be broken . – Yes, you're right. **I'll see the doctor**.*
3 *Can I use your phone? **I'm going to see the doctor**. I feel really ill.*
4 *Tomorrow I'll be in town at 5.30. **I'll see the doctor** at 6.00, so I'll get home at 7.00.*

● ***Going to*** **for imminent events** Check students' understanding of *going to* used in situations
where present evidence suggests an imminent future event or action.

Write on the board some leading sentences. Examples:
1 *That waiter's carrying too many plates.*   2 *Look at that car! He's driving too fast.*

Get the students to suggest sentences to follow the ones on the board. Examples:
1 *He's going to drop them. / They're going to fall.*
2 *He's going to crash. / He's going to hit that cyclist.*

Extension
● **Reference to the present** To help students to understand how we talk about the future, you can
explain that in most cases we're talking about the present and the future at the same time.

I'm going to buy a new dress.   (A plan, an intention I have <u>now</u>.)

She looks very unhappy – she's going to cry.   (A future event that seems certain because of
what we can see <u>now</u>.)

I'll have a coffee, please.   (A decision we make as we speak <u>now</u>.)

I'm leaving at 6.00 tomorrow.   (An arrangement I've already made –
I know <u>now</u> what I'm doing tomorrow.)

The exception is a simple prediction, where we say what will happen in the future. There is no
reference to the present: *The world will be very different in 2050.*

Answers to WHAT'S THE RULE? 6:
A 1 *Yes* 2 *a*   **B** *is ('s) going to buy*   **C** 1 *No* 2 *is ('s) going to*   **D** *will arrive*   **E** *b*
REMEMBER! 1d 2c 3b 4a 5e

Future: *going to* OR *will* OR present continuous?

My friend is going to live in Italy. That boat is going to sink – there are too many passengers.
Goodbye. I'll see you tomorrow. – I can't see you tomorrow. I'm playing tennis.

● **Future predictions**

Ask students to suggest what the world will be like in 25 years' time, using *will / won't*.

Examples:

I think people will live longer. There will be a cure for cancer.
People won't send ordinary letters – they'll use e-mail.
Europe's climate will be warmer.
More students will use computers to study.

● **Predictions and plans**

Ask students to write the following:

1 three simple predictions about the future.

Examples:
I think I'll pass my exams next month.
I'll get home at about 6.00 tonight.

2 three sentences about their plans/intentions for the future.

Examples:
I'm going to work this weekend.
I'm not going to get married.

Then students work in pairs and tell each other about their predictions and their intentions.

● **What's going to happen?**

Ask students to think of a sentence demonstrating the use of *going to* for imminent future events suggested by present evidence.

Then ask individual students to stand in front of the class and mime the actions that suggest what *he's/she's going to do*.

The rest of the class guess what's going to happen.

Examples:

A student mimes pumping up a bike tyre, then putting the pump away.
You're going to ride your bike.

A student mimes looking through, for example, a rack of clothes. He/she holds one or two items up against him/herself. Then he/she chooses one and mimes handing it to the assistant.
You're going to buy that sweater/blouse/jacket, etc.

● **A telephone call**

Students work in pairs and compose a short telephone conversation, using the present continuous and *will*. They're phoning a friend.

Example:
A: *Hello, can I speak to Carole?*
B: *I'm afraid she isn't here.*
A: *When will she be back?*
B: *I think she'll be back about 3.00.*
A: *OK. I'll phone again at about 3.30.*
B: *She won't be free at 3.30. She's having a guitar lesson.*
A: *OK. I'll phone this evening.*
B: *OK. I'll tell her you phoned.*

Answers to PRACTICE EXERCISES 6:
1 1e 2e 3a 4a 5d 6e 7b 8b + c   **2** 1 *will ('ll) be* 2 *am ('m) going to have* 3 *are coming* 4 *will ('ll) wear* 5 *isn't going to rain*
3 1 <u>I'm not working</u> 2 <u>I'm going to buy</u> 3 <u>She's working</u> 4 <u>I'll phone</u> 5 <u>We'll be</u>   **4** 1 *are you leaving* 2 *I'm getting* 3 *will you be*
4 *I'll come* 5 *I'm going to cry*

Future: *going to* OR *will* OR present continuous?

My friend is going to live in Italy. That boat is going to sink – there are too many passengers.
Goodbye. I'll see you tomorrow. – I can't see you tomorrow. I'm playing tennis.

1 Match the sentences with the explanations.

1 – Hi, Dan! What *are you doing* at the weekend? ☐ e

2 – *I'm staying* at home on Saturday. ☐

3 – What *are you going to do*? ☐

4 – *I'm going to revise* for my exams. ☐

5 – *Will you be* free on Saturday evening? ☐

6 – Yes, *I'm not doing* anything in the evening. ☐

7 – Good. We can watch the match on TV. *I'll come* at 7.30. ☐

8 – OK. *I'll see* you on Saturday. ☐

   I must go now. The cat's on the table. *It's going to eat* my dinner! ☐

a An intention, a plan made before the moment of speaking.
b An intention, a decision that we make now, at the moment of speaking.
c A future event or action that seems certain because of something we can see now.
d A simple future fact.
e An arrangement made for a particular time in the future.

2 What do you say? Use the present continuous or *will* or *going to*.

1 You're 16. It's your birthday next Friday.
   I (be) ......*will ('ll) be*...... 17 next Friday.

2 To celebrate your birthday, your parents wanted to take you to a restaurant, but yesterday you decided to have a big party.
   I don't want to go to a restaurant. I (have) .... a big party.

3 You've invited twenty people. They've all accepted the invitation. You're telling your parents about the arrangement.
   Twenty people (come) .... to my party.

4 You aren't sure what to wear on Friday. Decide!
   I know! I (wear) .... my white trousers.

5 You want to have the party outside. You're watching the TV weather forecast.
   Great! It (not rain) .... on Friday.

3 Which sentence follows the first sentence? <u>Underline</u> the correct verb form.

1 I'm free tomorrow. (<u>*I'm not working*</u>. / *I won't work.*)

2 I've decided to go into town. (*I'll buy* / *I'm going to buy* some new clothes.)

3 My sister can't come with me. (*She works* / *She's working* tomorrow morning.)

4 Who can I ask to go with me? I know! (*I'm going to phone* / *I'll phone* Kate.)

5 We can get the 8.30 bus. (*We'll be* / *We're going to be* in town at 9.00.)

4 This is a dialogue in a romantic film.
Complete the dialogue, using the present continuous (x 2), *will* (x 2) and *going to* (x 1).

– When (1 you leave) ......*are you leaving*...... ?

– Tomorrow. (2 I get) .... the 8.00 train.

– When (3 you be) .... back?

– In a year, two years – I don't know, but I promise (4 I come) .... back.

– Two years! Oh, Ralph, I'm so unhappy. (5 I cry) ....

🐱 **DESIGNED TO PHOTOCOPY**

Which tense after *when* in future sentences?

I'll phone you when I get home. I'll lend you the book when I have read it.

A

when-CLAUSE   MAIN CLAUSE

TOM: When I **leave** school next year, I**'ll** go round the world.

1 Is Tom talking about the present or the future? ....

2 Is *I leave* the present simple tense or a future tense? ....

Complete this rule, using the present simple or *will*:

In future sentences, we normally use .... in a *when*-clause.

B Now look at these sentences.

TOM: I'll get a job **as soon as I leave** school.   (NOT as soon as I ~~will leave~~)

I'll work **until I have** enough money.   (NOT until I ~~will have~~)

Before I go, I'll get a new passport.   (NOT Before I ~~will go~~)

While I am away, I'll e-mail my parents every week.   (NOT While I ~~will be~~)

Now complete this rule:

Like *when*, the time words *as soon as, until (till), after, before* and *while* are followed by a verb in the .... in future sentences. We don't use *will*.

C But look at these sentences, then answer the questions.

I need £1000 for my trip. I'll leave as soon as I**'ve saved** £1000.

1 Can Tom go with £750? ....

2 When can he go? As soon as .... £1000.

Now complete this rule:

If it's important to say that one action must be finished before the next action can start, we use the .... (*I've saved*) and not the ....
(*I save*) after *when, as soon as,* etc.

REMEMBER!

Complete these rules. Write *present simple, will* or *present perfect*.

1 In future sentences, we normally use the .... after *when, as soon as,* etc.

We don't use ....

2 But when it's important to make clear that one thing must be finished before the next thing can start, we use

the .... after *when, as soon as,* etc., and not the ....

Which tense after *when* in future sentences?

I'll phone you when I get home. I'll lend you the book when I have read it.

The problem: Students mistakenly use *will* for the future after time words like *when, as soon as, until, (till), after, before* and *while*.
They should use the present simple or the present perfect.

Typical mistakes: *When I'll be 18, I'll leave school.* (When I'm 18 …)
As soon as I'll get home this evening, I'll phone you. (As soon as I get …)
You can't go until you eat your breakfast. (until you've eaten …)

● **Present simple after *when*** Write this sentence on the board:
We'll have dinner when she comes.
Ask students if the speaker is talking about the present or the future.

Ask students: *What tense is **she comes**? (The present simple.)*

● **Think of examples** Explain that we use the present simple in clauses introduced by *when, as soon as, until, (till), after, before* and *while*. We do <u>not</u> use the *will* future.

Get students to work in groups. Each group should think of their own examples of future sentences containing *when, as soon as, until (till), after, before* and *while*.

Examples: *When I **leave** school, I'm going to be a model / an architect / a politician.*
*I won't get married until I**'m** 30.*

Students read out their sentences.

● **Present perfect after *when, as soon as,* etc.** Write this sentence on the board:
When we've had dinner, we'll go for a walk.
Ask students: *What tense is **we've had**? (The present perfect.)*

Ask students if this sentence is correct:
*When we **have** dinner, we'll go for a walk.*
(No. Because you can't have dinner and go for a walk at the same time!)

Explain that we use the present perfect after *when, as soon as,* etc. if it's important to emphasise that one action or event must be finished before another action is possible.

Write these examples on the board and get students to correct them:

When I'll save enough money, I'll buy a CD player. *(When I've saved …)*
I'll post this postcard as soon as I write it. *(… as soon as I've written it.)*

● **Complete the sentences** Write these clauses on the board:
I won't get married before … *… while I listen to the radio.*
My parents will be angry when … *… until I've had something to eat.*
I'll do my homework after … *… as soon as I have enough money.*

Students work in pairs and write complete sentences using each of the six clauses.
They then choose their 'best' sentences and read them to the class.

Examples: *My parents will be angry when they talk to my teacher.*
I won't start work until I've had something to eat.

Answers to WHAT'S THE RULE? 7:
A 1 *The future* **2** *The present simple* Rule: *the present simple* **B** *present simple* **C 1** *No* **2** *he's (has) saved* Rule: *present perfect; present simple*   **REMEMBER! 1** *present simple; will* **2** *present perfect; present simple*

Which tense after *when* in future sentences?

I'll phone you when I get home. I'll lend you the book when I have read it.

● **Correct the mistakes**

Write these sentences on the board.
All of them contain typical mistakes.
Students come to the board and correct the mistakes.

1 *As soon as it'll stop raining, we'll go out.*
(*As soon as it stops ...*)

2 *Phone me when you'll get there.*
(*... when you get there.*)

3 *Wait here until I'll get back.*
(*... until I get back.*)

4 *I'll write to my father when I'll have time.*
(*... when I have time.*)

5 *Before you'll leave, you must give me your address.*
(*Before you leave ...*)

6 *While we'll be away, can you look after our cat?*
(*While we're ...*)

● **When I get home!**

Students work in pairs. Together they write a dialogue between two ship-wrecked sailors on a desert island in which they talk about what they'll do when they're rescued. They should use as many of these words as possible, followed by the present simple or the present perfect: *when, as soon as, until (till), before, after, while*

Examples:
As soon as I get back *to England I'll put on some clean clothes!*
When I get back *I'll have a big dinner and* ***after I've eaten*** *I'll go to sleep in a real bed.*

● **Have a nice trip!**

Students work in groups. Each group decides on a trip they all want to make.

Examples:
Climbing in the Himalayas.
Shopping in New York.
Skiing in Switzerland.
Sailing in the Caribbean.

They then think of sentences, using as many of these words as possible, followed by the present simple or the present perfect: *when, as soon as, until (till), before, after, while*

Examples:
We won't go ***till*** *the weather* ***gets*** *warmer.*
While we're *there, we'll take lots of photographs.*
After we've visited *Central Park, we'll go to the top of the Empire State Building.*

● **After the party**

Students work in small groups. Together they think of different things that people at a party might say to each other as they leave.

They should use as many of these words as possible followed by the present simple or the present perfect: *when, while, as soon as, until (till), before, after.*

Examples:
I'll phone you ***as soon as I get up*** *tomorrow.*
I won't see you ***till I get back*** *from holiday.*
I'll see you ***when you come*** *into town tomorrow.*

Answers to PRACTICE EXERCISES 7:
1 1 <u>go</u> 2 <u>start</u> 3 <u>get</u> 4 <u>leave</u> 5 <u>arrive</u> 6 <u>am</u> 7 <u>leave</u>   **2** 1 <u>'ll (will) post</u> 2 <u>go</u> 3 <u>'ll (will) take</u> 4 <u>go</u> 5 <u>'ll (will) do</u>
6 *get back* 7 *'ll (will) tidy* 8 *finishes*   **3** 1 I'll leave *I leave* 2 ✔ 3 I'll be *I'm (am)* 4 I'll leave *I leave* 5 ✔ 6 I'll be *I'm (am)*
4 1 <u>I get</u> 2 <u>I'm</u> 3 <u>I've gone</u> 4 <u>I've made</u> 5 <u>I return</u> 6 <u>I come</u>

Which tense after *when* in future sentences?

I'll phone you when I get home. I'll lend you the book when I have read it.

1 Matthew is going on holiday to California next month.
<u>Underline</u> the correct alternative.

  1 I'll need a new passport before I *(go / will go)*.

  2 I'm going to leave as soon as my summer holidays *(start / will start)*.

  3 When I *(will get / get)* there, I think I'll rent a car.

  4 I'll change my pounds into dollars before I *(leave / will leave)*.

  5 I'm going to stay for a week in Los Angeles when I *(will arrive / arrive)*.

  6 While I *(will be / am)* there, I 'll stay in a motel.

  7 After I *(will leave / leave)* Los Angeles, I'm going to visit San Francisco.

2 Robert's 16. His mother's talking to him.
Put the verbs into the present simple or the *will* future.

MOTHER: Can you post this letter for me?

ROBERT: OK, I (1 post) ....*'ll (will) post*.......... it when I (2 go) .... out.

MOTHER: Can you take the dog for a walk?.

ROBERT: Yes, I (3 take) .... him with me when I (4 go) .... to John's.

MOTHER: Are you going to do any homework this evening?

ROBERT: Yes, I (5 do) .... it after I (6 get back) .... from John's.

MOTHER: Are you going to tidy your room or are you just going to watch TV?

ROBERT: I (7 tidy) .... my room as soon as this programme (8 finish) .... !

3 A French boy and a Japanese girl are talking about their future.
If the verb form is wrong, ~~cross it out~~ and write the correct form.
If the verb form is correct, put a tick (✔).

PASCAL:

  1 I'll probably go to university after ~~I'll leave~~ school.   ...*I leave*...........

  2 When I'm 25, I'll get married.   ....

  3 But I won't have any children till I'll be 30.   ....

YASUKO:

  4 As soon as I'll leave school, I'll get a job.   ....

  5 When I've saved enough money, I'll buy a car.   ....

  6 I'll live with my parents till I'll be 25.   ....

4 In a romantic film, the hero's speaking to Caroline, the woman he loves.
<u>Underline</u> the better alternative.

  1 I'll write to you as soon as *(I get / I'll get)* to Africa.

  2 And I'll think of you every day while *(I'm / I've been)* away.

  3 Will you think of me after *(I'll go / I've gone)*?

  4 When *(I've made / I make)* a lot of money, I'll come back.

  5 I'll ask you to marry me as soon as *(I'll return / I return)*.

  6 Oh Caroline, will you wait till *(I come / I'll come)* home?

8 WHAT'S THE RULE?

How do we form negatives?

Kate isn't happy because she hasn't found a job yet. I don't speak Japanese.
He didn't go to the party. You mustn't smoke. She can't swim.

A To form the negative of *is/are, was/were, have/has,* we add *not (n't).*
Fill in the gaps, using the correct negative form.

It's a national holiday today. Kate *isn't* going to school and her parents (1) .... going to work.

KATE: Great! *I'm not* going to get up till midday!

At 7.30 this morning there *wasn't* a queue at the bus-stop, and the streets (2) .... full of traffic.

It's 9.00 and Kate's father is waiting for two important letters. But they *haven't* arrived

because the postman (3) .... come. He *won't* get the letters until tomorrow.

Note these two forms:
I'm not going to school today.   (NOT I ~~amn't~~ going to school today.)
He won't get the letters until tomorrow.   (will + n't = won't NOT ~~willn't~~)

B With the present simple *(I eat)* we use *don't/doesn't.* With the past simple *(I went),* we use *didn't.*
Fill in the gaps, using the correct negative form.

Kate's vegetarian.   She *doesn't eat* meat.   (NOT She doesn't ~~eats~~ ...)

'I eat eggs and cheese.   But I (1) .... meat.'   (NOT I ~~eat not~~ ...)

She went out last night.   But she *didn't go* to a restaurant.   (NOT She didn't ~~went~~ ...)

She had a pizza at home.   But she (2) .... any ham.   (NOT She didn't ~~had~~ ...)

C The negative forms of *can* and *must.* Fill in the gaps, using the correct negative form.

Kate's revising for an important exam. She's going to work every evening next week.

She *can't* go to the cinema on Monday.   (NOT She ~~doesn't can~~ go ...)

'I (1) .... see my boyfriend on Tuesday.'   (NOT I ~~don't can~~ see ...)

She must revise. She *mustn't* go out next week.   (NOT She ~~doesn't must~~ go...)

'I must work hard. I (2) .... fail the exam.' (NOT I ~~don't must~~ fail ...)

D The negative word *never.*

Kate is very healthy. She's *never* ill. 'I *never* eat hamburgers or chips. And I've *never* smoked in my life.'

Write these sentences correctly:

1 I '~~m not never~~ ill.   I .... ill.

2 She ~~no has never smoked.~~   She ....

3 She ~~does never eat~~ hamburgers or chips. She .... hamburgers or chips.

REMEMBER!

Complete this table, using negative forms:

1 He's English.   ▶ She ..... *isn't* .... English.
2 He speaks English.   ▶ She .... English.
3 He can dance.   ▶ She ....
4 He was at the party. ▶ She .... at the party.
5 He went.   ▶ She ....
6 He always smiles.   ▶ She ....

DESIGNED TO PHOTOCOPY

How do we form negatives?

Kate isn't happy because she hasn't found a job yet. I don't speak Japanese.
He didn't go to the party. You mustn't smoke. She can't swim.

The problem: Many students find English negative forms difficult.
Typical mistakes: *I ~~no am~~ English.*   *I ~~like not~~ football.*

She ~~don't can~~ come.   *He doesn't ~~smokes~~.*   *I ~~no have~~ finished.*

He ~~not came~~ with me.   *He didn't ~~went~~ to the party.*

● **Negative forms** Write just the <u>full</u> forms on the board:

I am not	▶ *I'm not*	He has not	▶ *He hasn't / He's not*
She is not	▶ *She isn't / She's not*	She will not	▶ *She won't*
We are not	▶ *We aren't / We're not*	I would not	▶ *I wouldn't*
She was not	▶ *She wasn't*	She cannot	▶ *She can't*
They were not	▶ *They weren't*	I could not	▶ *I couldn't*
I have not	▶ *I haven't / I've not*	You must not	▶ *You mustn't*

Tell students that when we speak we don't normally use these full forms.
Ask them to say the short forms and to come and write them on the board. (If you like, you can
ask them to give the two possible short forms where this applies – see *Extensions* below.)

● ***Don't, doesn't, didn't*** Tell lies about yourself, using the present simple and the past simple!
Say the sentences on the left to the class. (You can of course choose other sentences, if you like.)
If students find a sentence difficult, write it on the board.

I live in Los Angeles.	*You **don't live** in Los Angeles.*
My father works in Hollywood.	*Your father **doesn't work** in Hollywood.*
My parents earn $500,000 a year.	*Your parents **don't earn** $500,000 a year.*
My father bought me a Cadillac yesterday.	*Your father **didn't buy** you a Cadillac yesterday.*
I went to Acapulco last week.	*You **didn't go** to Acapulco last week.*

After each sentence, get the class to contradict you, saying the negative sentences on the right.

● ***Can't* and *mustn't*** Remind students that we don't use *don't/doesn't* in the negative forms
of *can* and *must*.
Ask them to make negative sentences in response to some untrue prompts.
Example: *Maria can play the trumpet.* ▶ *She can't play the trumpet!* (NOT ~~don't can~~)
Then ask them to say what certain signs mean.
Example: *No smoking.* ▶ *You mustn't smoke.* (NOT ~~don't must~~)

Extensions

● **Two negative forms** Show students that with *is/are* and *have/has* there are two possible
negative forms:

*Kate **isn't** going to school.*	OR	*Kate**'s not** going to school.*
*She **isn't** going.*	OR	*She**'s not** going.*
*They **aren't** working.*	OR	*They**'re not** working.*
*They **haven't** arrived.*	OR	*They**'ve not** arrived.*

● **Negative commands** Remind students that we use *Don't* + infinitive to form a negative
command (imperative):   ***Don't** talk!*   ***Don't** sit there!*   ***Don't** do that!*   ***Don't** be silly!*

Answers to WHAT'S THE RULE? 8:
A 1 *aren't* **2** *weren't* **3** *hasn't*   **B 1** *don't eat* **2** *didn't have*   **C 1** *can't* **2** *mustn't*   **D 1** *'m never* **2** *has ('s) never smoked*
3 *never eats*   **REMEMBER! 1** *isn't* **2** *doesn't speak* **3** *can't dance* **4** *wasn't* **5** *didn't go* **6** *never smiles*

How do we form negatives?

Kate isn't happy because she hasn't found a job yet. I don't speak Japanese.
He didn't go to the party. You mustn't smoke. She can't swim.

● **Game: answer without saying *No*!**

A student stands in front of the class. The others ask him/her a lot of *Yes/No* questions. If he/she answers with the word 'No' then he/she loses the game and is replaced by another student. To avoid saying 'No', students have to answer with <u>full</u> negative sentences.

Examples:
Are you studying English?
(Yes.)

Do you like music?
(Yes.)

Are we speaking Spanish?
*(You **aren't speaking** Spanish.)*

Does Anna play the trumpet?
*(She **doesn't play** the trumpet.)*

Will Roberto be 20 next year?
*(He **won't be** 20 next year.)*

● **That's a lie!**

Students work in pairs. Student A tells several lies, using an affirmative sentence. Student B contradicts what his/her partner says.

Examples:
A: *I can speak ten languages.*
B: *You **can't speak** ten languages!*
A: *I'm very, very intelligent.*
B: *You **aren't** very intelligent!*
A: *I went to the Antarctic last summer.*
B: *You **didn't go** to the Antarctic!*

Student A and Student B then change roles.

● **Listen and correct**

Read a short text to the class. Let the students hear it at least twice. Then talk about the details of the text, making some deliberate mistakes. Students will recognise the mistakes and should correct them, using a negative sentence.

Example:
David lives in Oxford. He'll be 19 next week. He's got long blond hair and he wears black boots. He's a musician. He plays the guitar in a band. Last week the band played at a big concert in London. There were 2,000 people there. The concert started at 8.30 and it finished at 11.45.

David lives in London.
*(No, he **doesn't live** in London.*
He lives in Oxford.)

He's got short dark hair.
*(No, he **hasn't got** short dark hair.*
He's got long blond hair.)

He wears brown boots.
*(No, he **doesn't wear** brown boots.*
He wears black boots.)

There were 3,000 people at the concert.
*(No, there **weren't** 3,000 people.*
There were 2,000.)

and so on.

How do we form negatives?

Kate isn't happy because she hasn't found a job yet. I don't speak Japanese.
He didn't go to the party. You mustn't smoke. She can't swim.

1 Gerry has got very little money, no job and no home. He lives on the streets of London.
Rewrite these sentences in the negative to tell the truth about him.

1 He's got a lot of money.   *He hasn't got a lot of money.* ....

2 He lives in a big house. ....

3 He <u>always</u> wears expensive clothes. ....

4 He went to Miami in April. ....

5 He was in Brazil in May. ....

6 He'll be in Thailand next month. ....

7 He's been all over the world. ....

8 He can speak five languages. ....

9 He's very happy. ....

2 Look at the pictures. Write <u>negative</u> sentences about each picture.
Use these verbs: *need, rain, be (x 4), can (x 2), buy, wear, shine, like, see, have got*

1 He ....*doesn't need*........ his umbrella because
it .... There ....
any taxis.

2 She .... the dress because the
shop .... open. The dress ....
very expensive.

3 He .... his sun hat because the
sun .... He ....
the food.

4 He .... very well because he
.... tall enough. He ....
a very good seat.

3 Complete these short dialogues, using negative verbs (*isn't, don't, can't*, etc.)

TOURIST: Excuse me. Can you help me? I (1) ...*don't*.... know the way to the station.

PASSER-BY: I'm afraid I (2) .... help you. I (3) .... sure where the station is. I (4) .... live here.

SARAH: Did you go shopping yesterday?

JENNY: Yes, but I (5) .... buy anything. I saw some nice shoes, but they (6) .... my size.
They were too small. I tried them, but I (7) .... get them on.

MIKE: Hello? Can I speak to Kim, please?

HELEN: I'm afraid she (8) .... here. I (9) .... seen her today. I think she's at work.
So she (10) .... be back till 6.30.

How do we form questions?

Why are you crying? What do you mean? Who did you talk to?

A Questions with *am/are/is, was/were* (the verb *be*).

SUBJECT   VERB
He   is   Italian.
VERB   SUBJECT
Is   ***he***   Italian?

SUBJECT   VERB
His parents   are   in England.
VERB   SUBJECT
Are   ***his parents***   in England?

Anna's asking Lisa about her new boyfriend. Put her questions in the right order.

1 he a student is? ....?   **2** he was at Joe's party? ....?

3 how old he is? ....?   **4** his friends are nice? ....?

B Questions with an auxiliary verb (*is/are/was/were/have/can/will*, etc.) + main verb.

SUBJECT   AUXILIARY   MAIN VERB
Anna   is   talking   to Lisa.
AUXILIARY   SUBJECT   MAIN VERB
Is   ***Anna***   ***talking***   to Lisa?

Put Anna's questions in the right order.

1 he is studying English? ....?

2 he in England has lived long? ....?

3 his parents you have met? ....?

4 what time you are meeting him tonight? ....?

5 he drive can? ....?

6 you will go where? ....?

C To form questions in the present simple (*I like*), we use *do* or *does* + the infinitive.

Do you *like* him?   (NOT ~~Like you~~ him? OR ~~You like~~ him?)
Does he *smoke*?   (NOT ~~Smokes he~~? OR ~~He smokes~~?)
What ***do*** his friends ***think***?   (NOT What ~~think his friends~~? OR What ~~his friends~~ think?)

Rewrite Anna's questions correctly.

1 He likes you? ....   **2** Why you like him? ....

3 Where he lives? ....   **4** Where live his parents? ....

D To form questions in the past simple (*I saw*), we use *did* + the infinitive.

Did you *see* him yesterday?   (NOT ~~Saw you~~ him yesterday? OR ~~You saw~~ him yesterday?)

Rewrite Anna's questions correctly.

1 Where you went? ....?   **2** You enjoyed the film? ....?

3 Roberto took you home? ....?

REMEMBER!

Choose an example sentence from this page for each rule.

1 To form questions with auxiliaries like *are/is, was/were, have/has, can/will*, etc, we put the auxiliary before the subject. Example: ....

2 To form questions in the present simple, we put *do* or *does* before the infinitive form of the verb.

Example: ....

3 To form questions in the past simple, we put *did* before the infinitive.

Example: ....

How do we form questions?

Why are you crying? What do you mean? Who did you talk to?

The problem: Students aren't sure of the correct word order in questions, and the use of *do, does* and *did* causes difficulty.

Typical mistakes: ~~You are~~ English? Why ~~you are~~ late? What ~~you want~~? Where ~~he work~~?
Does she ~~knows~~? ~~Do you can~~ swim? ~~Came Tom?~~ Did they ~~went~~? ~~It has~~ stopped?

● **Basic question forms** Tell students that a detective is interviewing a suspected criminal, Carl Mason. The detective knows the following facts about Mason. Write them on the board (but not the questions on the right).

He is from east London.	(***Are you*** from east London?)
He was in the Oasis club last night.	(***Were you*** in the Oasis club last night?)
He hasn't got a job.	(***Have you got*** a job?)
He has bought a new BMW.	(***Have you bought*** a new BMW?)
He knows a drug dealer called Sid	(***Do you know*** a drug dealer called Sid?)
Sid gives him money.	(***Does Sid give*** you money?)
He met Sid last night.	(***Did you meet*** Sid last night?)

Tell students that the detective wants to check these facts.
Tell them to write down the detective's questions (in brackets above).

Get individual students to come to the board and write one question at a time.
Discuss any mistakes and encourage students to correct each other.

Remind students of the basic rules:

THE VERB *be*: He is from east London.   He was in the Oasis club last night.

Is he from east London?   ***Was he*** in the Oasis club last night?

AUXILIARY + MAIN VERB: He has bought a new BMW.

Has he ***bought*** a new BMW?

PRESENT SIMPLE: You know Sid.   ▶ ***Do you know*** Sid?
Sid gives him money.   ▶ ***Does Sid give*** him money?

PAST SIMPLE: He met Sid last night.   ▶ ***Did he meet*** Sid last night?

● **Correcting common mistakes** Write these incorrect question forms on the board and get students to correct them.

Carl is from London?	What do Sid give him?
Where Carl was last night?	When he met Sid?
He has got a job?	Did he met him at the club?
What he has bought?	What they were talking about?
Does he knows Sid?	

Answers to WHAT'S THE RULE? 9:
A 1 *Is he a student?* 2 *Was he at Joe's party?* 3 *How old is he?* 4 *Are his friends nice?* **B** 1 *Is he studying English?* 2 *Has he lived in England long?* 3 *Have you met his parents?* 4 *What time are you meeting him tonight?* 5 *Can he drive?* 6 *Where will you go?*
C 1 *Does he like you?* 2 *Why do you like him?* 3 *Where does he live?* 4 *Where do his parents live?* **D** 1 *Where did you go?*
2 *Did you enjoy the film?* 3 *Did Roberto take you home?*
REMEMBER! 1 *Is he Italian?*, etc. 2 *Do you like him?*, etc. 3 *Did you see him yesterday?*, etc.

How do we form questions?

Why are you crying? What do you mean? Who did you talk to?

● **General knowledge questions**

Students work in groups. Each group writes ten general knowledge questions using a variety of tenses. Move round the class checking that the questions are correctly formed.

Examples:
Is New York the capital of the USA?
Where are the Seychelles?
When did man first land on the moon?
Does Great Britain have a president?
Where will the next Olympics be?
Has Spain ever won the World Cup?

One student in each group reads out a question. The rest of the class try to answer it.

● **What's wrong?**

Read out the following incorrect question forms, or think of your own. Students should correct them as quickly as possible by shouting out the correct form.
You speak English?
Is raining?
Where you are going?
She likes me?
Why you laughing?
Do you can come?
How much it costs?
What means this word?
When they did leave?
Where did you went yesterday?
You go to the party next Saturday?

● **Make changes**

Say the following sentence:
Do you speak English?

Go round the class getting each student to say the sentence, changing one word and substituting a different word.

Examples:
Do you speak Italian? ▶ *Do you **understand** Italian?* ▶ *Do you understand **computers**?* ▶ *Do **girls** understand computers?* ▶ *Do girls understand **boys**?* ▶ *Do girls **interest** boys?* etc.

● **What were the questions?**

Students form two teams. Write these answers on the board, one at a time.
English.   No, I don't.   At 3 o'clock.
Yes, I can.   No, she wasn't.   No, he doesn't.
Yes, I have.   In bed.   Yesterday.   Yellow.
New York.   30 kilometres.   In May.
Because I was bored.

The two teams take it in turns to think of different questions for each answer. They get a point for each correct question. If they make a mistake or take longer than five seconds, the other team get a point.

Example:
English.
A: *What nationality was Shakespeare?*
B: *What language do they speak in Australia?*

How do we form questions?

Why are you crying? What do you mean? Who did you talk to?

1 A Greek student and a German student are at a language school in Oxford.
The Greek student is asking a lot of questions. Put the words in the right order.

1 you from are where? ..... *Where are you from?* .....

2 do in Germany live where you? .....

3 you living where are in Oxford? .....

4 at school did learn you English? .....

5 have how long been in England you? .....

6 been to London you have? .....

7 this evening what do you to are going? .....

2 Louise is applying for a new job. What are the interviewer's questions?

1 What ..... *'s your name* ..... ? My name's Louise.

2 How ..... ? I'm 19.

3 Where ..... ? I live in Clifton.

4 ..... at home? Yes, I'm still living with my parents.

5 When ..... ? I left school a year ago.

6 Which ..... to? I went to Backwell school.

7 ..... a job? Yes, I've got a job as a receptionist.

8 How long ..... ? I've had the job for a year.

3 Complete these questions at a railway station.

1 When / the next train to Cambridge / leave? It leaves at 10.20.
When does the next train to Cambridge leave?
.....

2 What time / now? It's 10.10.
.....

3 What time / get / to Cambridge? It gets to Cambridge at 11.43.
.....

4 I / have to / change? No, you don't have to change.
.....

5 How much / a return ticket / cost? It costs £26.50.
.....

6 pay / by credit card? Yes, you can pay by Visa or Mastercard.
.....

4 A police officer in Mexico asks an American tourist these questions.
If the question form is wrong, write the correct form. If it is correct, put a tick (✔).

1 What nationality you are? *What nationality are you?* .....

2 What's your name? .....

3 You are a tourist? .....

4 Where you are staying? .....

5 You know the address of the hotel? .....

6 Where you lost your passport? .....

Active OR passive?

I make my own clothes. This car is made in Mexico. Who wrote this song? – It was written by an American singer.

A

ACTIVE
1 Fiona *cleans* her car every week.

PASSIVE
2 The manager's car *is cleaned* every week.

In which sentence, 1 or 2, are we interested in the action <u>and</u> the person who does the action? ☐

In which sentence are we interested only in the action? ☐

In Sentence 2, do we know who cleans the manager's car? ....

In Sentence 2, is it important to know who cleans the manager's car? ....

B

ACTIVE
1 This truck *hit* Fiona's car.

PASSIVE
2 Her car *was hit* by a truck.

In which sentence are we interested in the truck <u>and</u> what happened to Fiona's car? ☐

In which sentence are we more interested in the thing that hit her car? ☐

Note that in a passive sentence we use *by* if we want to say who or what does the action.

C Look at these pairs of sentences. <u>Underline</u> the 'better' sentence, *a* or *b*.

1 a Fiona phoned the police.   **b** The police were phoned by Fiona.

2 a A man will repair her car tomorrow.   **b** Her car will be repaired tomorrow.

3 a Fiona's car was made in Japan.   **b** Some people in Japan made Fiona's car.

REMEMBER!

Match the four sentences with the rules:

1 *Fiona's car radio was stolen yesterday.* ☐

2 *She didn't see the thief.* ☐

3 *2,000 car radios are stolen every week in Britain.* ☐

4 *Many are stolen by children under the age of 15.* ☐

a We use an active verb when we're interested in the action and who does it.

b We use a passive verb when we're more interested in the action, when we don't know who does the action or when it isn't important to say who does it.

c We can give extra information after a passive verb and say who does the action.

40

Active OR passive?

I make my own clothes. This car is made in Mexico. Who wrote this song? – It was written by an American singer.

The problem: A passive construction is often used in English where in other languages people would use an active construction.

Examples: *English is spoken in many parts of the world.* (NOT ~~One speaks~~ English ...)
These computers are sold all over Britain. (NOT Computers ~~sell themselves~~ ...)
The film can be seen on TV tomorrow. (NOT ~~One can~~ see ...)

● **Use of the passive** Tell the class that last year you stayed at a luxury hotel.
Say the following sentences, and write perhaps two on the board.
My suitcase was carried to my room. My bed was made. My clothes were washed.
My shoes were polished. My room was cleaned. My meals were served in my room.

Ask: *What is important in these sentences – the things that happened*
OR *who did them? (The things that happened.)*

Ask: *Are the verbs in the sentences active or passive? Why are they passive?*
(They're passive. Because we're interested in the actions, not in the people who did them.)

● **Use of *by*** Say this sentence to the class: *An old lady found my passport in the street.*
Ask: *Who found my passport?* Tell students to answer with a passive construction.
*(It **was found** by an old lady.)*

Say other similar sentences. Examples:
*A lot of tourists visit the cathedral. (Who visits the cathedral? It**'s visited** by a lot of tourists.)*
*Picasso painted this picture. (Who painted the picture? It **was painted** by Picasso.)*

● **Different tenses in the passive** Write only the active sentences in the left-hand column
on the board:

They've found some dinosaur bones. *(Some dinosaur bones **have been found**.)*
They showed them on TV last night. *(They **were shown** on TV last night.)*
They'll examine the bones tomorrow. *(The bones **will be examined** tomorrow.)*
You don't often find them in England. *(They **aren't** often **found** in England.)*

Ask students: *Are these sentences active or passive? (Active.)*
But do we know exactly who does these actions? (No.) Is that important? (No.)

Ask: *So, can you say these sentences in a different way? (Yes.)*
Now get students to tell you the equivalent passive constructions (see right-hand column).

Extension

● **Informal or formal sentences** Explain to students that in informal English, instead of using
a passive construction, we often use *we, you, they* with an active verb to refer to people
in general, to people in authority or to unknown people.

INFORMAL
***We use** a lot of antibiotics in England.*
***You can buy** tickets at the entrance.*
***They've found** the missing girl.*

FORMAL
▶ *A lot of antibiotics are used in England.*
▶ *Tickets can be bought at the entrance.*
▶ *The missing girl has been found.*

Answers to WHAT'S THE RULE? 10:
A 1; 2; *No; No.* **B** 1; 2 **C** 1a 2b 3a **REMEMBER!** 1 b 2a 3b 4c

Active OR passive?

I make my own clothes.   This car is made in Mexico.   Who wrote this song? – It was written by an American singer.

● **Write a news report**

Students work in groups and write a news bulletin with three or four items of news. *(Damage caused by severe weather, a traffic accident, a robbery, a plan for new hospitals/sports centres/roads, etc.)*

Students should use a mixture of active and passive sentences.

Help each group with vocabulary (write the words they need on the board).

Examples:
*Storms **have caused** a lot of damage on the coast. (Active)*
*Villages **have been flooded**. The road from X to Y **has been closed**. (Passive)*
*Many houses **have been damaged** by the wind. (Passive)*

*A bus carrying 30 tourists **hit** a bridge on the motorway last night. (Active)*
*Three people **were hurt** in the accident. (Passive)*
*An ambulance **was called**. The three tourists **were taken** to hospital. (Passive)*

Each group then chooses a speaker who reads the news bulletin to the class.

● **What happens there?**

Write these places on the board (or choose others if you like):
a travel agent's   McDonald's   an Internet cafe   a stadium   a garage

The class forms two teams, A and B. Each team in turn gives a passive sentence or an active sentence (using *'you'*), to describe the first place. Give a point for each correct sentence. When the two teams can't think of any more sentences, move on to the next place.

Examples:
A travel agent's is a place where holidays are arranged/where you can buy plane tickets.

McDonald's is a place where you can buy food/where hamburgers are sold.

An Internet café is a place where the Internet can be used/where you can send an e-mail.

● **What has been done?**

Get the students to look at the two pictures in PRACTICE EXERCISES 10 (Exercise 5).

If necessary, explain some of the vocabulary first: *drawer, wastepaper bin*, etc.

Then ask students to make two sentences about each thing that has happened in Picture 2. One sentence should be active, one passive. (They should use the present perfect tense because we're talking about the present results of a past action.)

Examples:
They've made the bed. + The bed has been made.
They've turned the TV off. + The TV has been turned off.

Answers to PRACTICE EXERCISES 10:
1 1 *False* 2 *True*   **2** 2 ✔ 4 ✔; 1 *A lot of changes have been made in the village.* 3 *The old school is used as a sports centre.*
3 1 *When were the pyramids built?* 2 *Is Spanish spoken in Brazil?* 3 *What languages are spoken in India?* 4 *Has any life been found on Mars?* 5 *Where will the next World Cup be played?* 6 *When was television invented?* 7 *Where is coffee grown?*
4 1 *cyclist was hit by a bus* 2 *was a fire* 3 *will be opened by* 4 *attacked a girl* 5 *was attacked by* 6 *will be shown*
5 *They've made the bed. / The bed has been made. They've turned the TV off. / The TV has been turned off. They've cleaned the floor. / The floor has been cleaned. They've opened the windows. / The windows have been opened. They've emptied the wastepaper bin. / The wastepaper bin has been emptied. They've closed the drawers. / The drawers have been closed. They've cleaned the glasses. / The glasses have been cleaned.*

Active OR passive?

I make my own clothes. This car is made in Mexico. Who wrote this song? – It was written by an American singer.

1 Write *True* or *False*.

We use the passive when we're more interested ...

1 in the person who does the action than in the action.   ....…

2 in the action than in the person who does it.   ....…

2 Put a tick (✔) by the sentences that are in the passive.

1 They have made a lot of changes in the village. ☐   3 They use the old school as a sports centre. ☐

2 A new primary school was built last year. ☐   4 100 new houses will be built next year. ☐

Now rewrite the sentences that are active, using a passive sentence.

....

....

3 Rewrite these general questions, using a question in the passive.

1 When did they build the pyramids?   *When were the pyramids built?* ....

2 Do they speak Spanish in Brazil?   ....

3 What languages do they speak in India?   ....

4 Have they found any life on Mars?   ....

5 Where will they play the next World Cup?   ....

6 When did they invent television?   ....

7 Where do they grow coffee?   ....

4 These are some headlines in a local newspaper. Write a full version of each headline.
Say what happened or what will happen, using an active or passive form, as necessary.
Use these verbs: *hit, be, show, attack (x 2), open*

1 BUS HITS CYCLIST   A ....*cyclist was hit by a bus*.......................... in the High Street.

2 FIRE AT HILL HOTEL   There .... at the Hill Hotel last night.

3 MAYOR TO OPEN NEW CINEMA   A new cinema .... the mayor next week.

4 DOG ATTACKS GIRL IN PARK   A dog .... in the park yesterday.

5 MAN ATTACKED BY PET SNAKE   A man .... his pet python last night.

6 CARNIVAL TO BE SHOWN ON NATIONAL TV   Next week's carnival .... on national TV.

5 Describe picture 2 of the hotel room, using the active and the passive.

11 WHAT'S THE RULE?

When do we use *will* in *if*-sentences?

If I have a headache, I drink a lot of water. If I miss the bus, I'll be late for school.
If you go to London, you might see the Queen.

A *If* + PRESENT + PRESENT SIMPLE

If you **want** to catch a fish, you **need** patience.

If Steve **has** time, he always **goes** fishing at the weekend.

If it**'s raining**, he **sits** under an umbrella.

These are facts or things that are always true.
Now complete this sentence.

If he (be) .... busy,

Steve (not go) .... fishing.

B *If* + PRESENT + *will / won't*

Steve's fishing. He's thinking about what will possibly happen.

If I**'m** lucky, I**'ll** catch a big fish.   (NOT If I'll be ....)

If I **catch** a big fish, we**'ll** have it for dinner tonight.   (NOT If I'll catch ...)

If I **go** home without a fish, my wife **won't** be pleased.   (NOT If I'll go ....)

These are two more future possibilities. Complete the sentences.

1 If he (not catch) .... a fish soon, he (move) .... to a different place.

2 If he (catch) .... a small fish, he (put) .... it back in the water.

C *If* + PRESENT + MODAL VERB

We can also use a modal verb *(may/might/can/must)* in the main clause.

If he **wants** to catch a fish, he **must** be patient.

If he **doesn't catch** a fish today, he **may** come back tomorrow.

Complete this sentence.

If he (not catch) .... a fish soon, he (might + go) .... home.

D *If* **can come at the beginning or in the middle of the sentence. The meaning is the same.**

If he catches a big fish, he'll be happy. OR He'll be happy *if* he catches a big fish.

Rewrite this sentence.

If it doesn't stop raining, I'll go home.

....

┌─ **REMEMBER!** ─┐
Complete these rules:

1 We use *If* + present + ... for things that are always true.

2 We use *If* + ... + *will / won't* when we talk about real future possibilities.

3 We can also use *If* + present simple + a modal verb, like *may*, ... , ... , ...

4 We do not use .... (the future tense) in the *if*-clause.

44

When do we use *will* in *if*-sentences?

If I have a headache, I drink a lot of water. If I miss the bus, I'll be late for school.
If you go to London, you might see the Queen.

The problem:	Students are not sure which tense to use after *if* when they are talking about a real possibility in the future. They often think that because they are talking about the future, they should use a future tense.
Typical mistakes:	*If ~~it'll stop~~ raining, we'll go out.* (If it stops ...)
	If the phone ~~will ring,~~ I'll answer it. (If the phone rings ...)

● **Facts that are always true** Tell the class what you normally do in the evening.
Write this sentence on the board:
If I feel tired, I don't go out in the evening.
Underline the two verbs and ask: *What tense are the two verbs in? (The present simple.)*
Ask students to think of other examples of *If* + present simple/continuous + present simple
for facts or things that are always true.
Examples: *If I go to bed late on Saturday, I get up late on Sunday morning.*
            If I'm studying for an exam, I go to bed early.

● **Future possibilities** Now tell students what you're thinking of doing this evening.
Write these two sentences on the board:
1 *If there's a good film on television, I'll watch it.*
2 *If there isn't, I'll go out with some friends.*
Ask: *Am I talking about the present or the future? (The future.)*
Give students these three alternatives. Ask them to choose the one that explains
the meaning of the two sentences.
a *There will definitely be a good film on TV this evening.*
b *There is a real possibility that there is a good film on TV this evening.*
c *It is very improbable or impossible that there is a good film on TV this evening.*
Underline the two verbs in the *if-* clause in each sentence (*If there's* and *If there isn't*).
Ask: *What tense are both these verbs in? (The present simple.)*

● **Position of the *if*-clause** Rewrite the second example on the board like this:
I'll go out with some friends if there isn't a good film on TV.
Ask: *Is there any difference in meaning between the two sentences? (No, there isn't.)*
Get students to give you their own examples of what they're thinking of doing this evening,
using this structure: *If* + present + *will/won't* OR *will/won't* + *if* + present

● **Modal verbs in the main clause** Tell students more about what you're thinking of doing this
evening. Choose examples, using a modal verb *(may/might/can/must)* in the main clause.
Examples: *If I go out with friends, we **might** go to the cinema.*
            *If we go to a bar, I **mustn't** stay too late.*

● **Correcting typical mistakes** Write these typical mistakes on the board. Get students to correct them.
If you'll post the letter today, she'll get it tomorrow. (If you post ...)
If they won't play well, they won't win. (If they don't play well, ...)
She might pass the exam if she'll work hard. (... if she works hard.)

When do we use *will* in *if*-sentences?

If I have a headache, I drink a lot of water. If I miss the bus, I'll be late for school.
If you go to London, you might see the Queen.

● **Future possibilities**

Write this list of future possibilities on the board:
I might go out this evening.
I might go shopping tomorrow.
The weather might be fine next weekend.
It might rain next weekend.

Students write sentences with *if* + the present + *will/won't* for each possibility.

Example:
If I go out this evening, I'll go to the cinema.
Students then work in pairs and try to guess what their partner has written for each possibility. Finally, they can compare what they have written.

● **A trip to the USA**

Write on the board: *If I go to the USA ...*

Tell students you want them to think about real possibilities in the future. Give them a few minutes to think about what they'll do or what they might do, if they go to the USA.

Ask students for their ideas.

Examples:
If I go to the USA, I'll spend a week in New York.
If I go to the USA, I'll visit California.
If I go to the USA, I might watch a baseball match.

Finally ask students to try and remember what other members of the class will do.

Example:
If Luis goes to the USA, he'll visit the Grand Canyon.

● **Warnings**

Ask students to think about mistakes which they have made in the past. Give an example:
When I was 18, I used to drive too fast. I had a bad accident.

Tell the class what you've learnt from your mistake and give them a warning:
If you drive too fast, you'll have an accident.

Tell students to write their own similar warnings and to read them out to the class.

Examples:
I drank too much last night. I've got a headache this morning.
If you drink too much, you'll have a headache the next day.

● **A letter to an English friend**

Students work in small groups. They imagine they're writing to an English friend who's coming to stay with them. Together they think of ways of ending these sentences:
If you come in July, ...
If you like sport, ...
We can go to X if you ....
We won't go to museums or art galleries if ....
If you're interested in X, we'll ....
If the weather's good, we'll ....

Answers to PRACTICE EXERCISES 11:
1 1 *'s/is; 'll/will go;* b   2 *'s/is; go;* a   3 *'s/is; might go;* c   **2** 1 *If you're a nurse, you don't earn much money.*   2 *If you're a barman, you meet a lot of people.*   3 *If you're a politician, you don't always tell the truth.*   4 *If you're a pilot, you aren't afraid of flying.*
5 *If you're a writer, you drink a lot of coffee.*   **3** 1e 2f 3d 4c 5a 6b   **4** 1 *goes; won't/will not sleep*   2 *'ll/will watch; let*
3 *don't let; 'll/will want*   4 *read; 'll/will go*   5 *'re/are; won't/will not wake up*   6 *can give; wakes up*   7 *'ll/will find; want*   8 *'s/is; might get*
5 1 ~~I'll never see~~ *I never see*   2 ~~you'll come~~ *you come*   3 ~~you'll phone~~ *you phone*   4 ~~you'll write~~ *you write*   5 ~~you'll find~~ *you find*

When do we use *will* in *if*-sentences?

If I have a headache, I drink a lot of water. If I miss the bus, I'll be late for school.
If you go to London, you might see the Queen.

1 Complete the sentences, using the correct verb forms. Then match the sentences with the explanations.

1 If it (be) ....*is*......... hot tomorrow, I (go) .... to the beach. ☐

2 If it (be) .... hot, I always (go) .... to the beach. ☐

3 If it (be) .... hot tomorrow, I (might + go) .... to the beach. ☐

a This is a habit; it's always true.
b This is a real possibility.
c This is a possibility, but the speaker isn't sure what he'll do.

2 Put these facts about different jobs into sentences with *if* + present + present simple.

1 Nurses don't earn much money.   *If you're a nurse, you don't earn much money.*
....

2 Barmen meet a lot of people.   ....

3 Politicians don't always tell the truth.   ....

4 Pilots aren't afraid of flying.   ....

5 Writers drink a lot of coffee.   ....

3 Two parents are talking about their son who's in his last year at school. Match the two parts of the sentences.

1 If he goes out every night, ☐ *e*   **a** he won't listen.

2 If he doesn't work harder, ☐   **b** if you speak to him.

3 He won't go to university, ☐   **c** he'll get a better job.

4 But if he goes to university, ☐   **d** if he doesn't pass the exam.

5 If I speak to him, ☐   **e** he won't do enough work.

6 But he'll listen to you ☐   **f** he won't pass the exam.

4 Katherine's going out this evening. She's talking to the babysitter who's going to look after Zoe, her 3 year-old daughter. Put the verbs into the correct tense.

1 If Zoe (go) ......*goes*............... to bed early, she (not sleep) ...*won't sleep*............

2 She (watch) .... TV all evening if you (let) .... her.

3 If you (not let) .... her watch TV, she (want) .... a story instead.

4 And if you (read) .... her a story, she (go) .... to sleep.

5 If you (be) .... lucky, she (not wake up) ....

6 You (can + give) .... her a drink if she (wake up) ....

7 You .... (find) coffee and tea in the kitchen if you .... (want) a drink.

8 If there (be) .... a lot of traffic, I (might + get) .... home late.

5 Carmen doesn't want to see her boyfriend again.
~~Cross out~~ the mistakes in these sentences and write the correct form.

1 If ~~I'll never see~~ you again, I won't be sorry.   *I never see*
....

2 If you'll come to my house, I won't answer the door.   ....

3 I won't speak to you if you'll phone me   ....

4 If you'll write to me, I won't reply.   ....

5 If you'll find my old letters, you can burn them.   ....

When do we use *would* in *if*-sentences?

If we had a car, the journey would be easier. If I lived near the sea, I could go to the beach every day.

A

PRESENT SIMPLE   +   *will*
1 If it *rains* this afternoon, Joe *will be* angry.

PAST SIMPLE   +   *would*
2 If it *rained* this afternoon, Stella *would be* pleased.

In both sentences we're talking about the same time – the future. (We are <u>not</u> talking about the past in the second sentence.) So why are the sentences different?

In which sentence is it improbable that it will rain this afternoon? ☐

In which sentence is there a real possibility that it will rain this afternoon? ☐

B Stella has to leave home at 6.15 a.m.

STELLA: I can't leave later.
           If I *left* home at 6.30, I*'d be* late for college.
           I *wouldn't walk* to college if I *had* a car.

Stella doesn't usually leave home at 6.30.
She doesn't have a car.
So, is she talking about (a) real possibilities or (b) improbable situations? ☐

C JOE: I*'d play* tennis every day if I *wasn't* at college.
         If I *was* a professional tennis player, my life *would be* really exciting.

Joe is at college. He isn't a professional tennis player.
So, is he talking about (a) real possibilities or (b) imaginary situations? ☐

Note that *if* can come at the beginning or in the middle of the sentence:
I*'d play* tennis every day if I *wasn't* at college. OR If I *wasn't* at college, I*'d play* tennis every day.

D *If + SIMPLE PAST + might / could*

We often use *might* (= *perhaps I would*) and *could* (= *would be able to*) in *if*-sentences.

     JOE: *If* I *had* tennis lessons every day, I *might* be World Number 1 one day.
STELLA: *If* someone *gave* me $1000, I *could* buy a car.

REMEMBER!

Complete these rules:

1 We use the 1st conditional *If* + …………........…………................……... + *will* (*'ll*) to talk about future situations
that are real possibilities.

2 We use the 2nd conditional *If* + …………........…………................……... + *would* (*'d*) to talk about future situations
that are improbable, unreal or imaginary.

When do we use *would* in *if*-sentences?

If we had a car, the journey would be easier. If I lived near the sea, I could go to the beach every day.

The problem: Students often make mistakes with tenses in the *if*-clause and the main clause. In particular, they mistakenly use *will/would* in the *if*-clause.

Typical mistakes:
If I ~~will go~~ to London, I will go by train.   (If I go …)
If I ~~would live~~ in the country, I'd be happier.   (If I lived …)
If I had enough money, I'~~ll buy~~ a car.   (… I'd buy …)
If I ~~have~~ a better job, I'd be happier.   (If I had …)

● **Difference between 1st and 2nd conditional** Describe a <u>present</u> problem where you are trying to decide what to do. You want to visit a friend in a town called X. You could go by train, by bus or by plane. First, write these facts on the board:
If I go by train, it'll take three hours. If I go by bus, it'll take five hours.
If I go by plane, it'll take an hour.
Ask students: *Am I thinking about real possibilities or improbable situations?*
        (Real possibilities. These are the real journey times.)
Write on the board: Real possibilities = 1st conditional (*If* + present simple + *will*)
Then tell students that you haven't got much money at the moment, and you don't like travelling by bus, because it makes you feel ill. Write these sentences on the board:
1 *If I went by plane, it would be too expensive.*   **2** *If I went by bus, I'd feel ill.*
Ask students: *So, how will I get to X? (You'll go by train.)*
Say: *So, in sentences 1 and 2 am I thinking about real possibilities or very improbable situations?*
    (Very improbable situations.)
Then write on the board: Improbable situations = 2nd conditional (*If* + past simple + *would*).

● **Checking the difference** Write these two sentences on the board:
1 *If I meet the President, I'll ask him to cut taxes.*   **2** *If I met the President, I'd ask him to cut taxes.*
Ask: *Who said each sentence – a factory worker, or a member of the National Congress?*
    (1 *A member of the National Congress.* 2 *A factory worker.*)
Get students to explain their choice. Then write these two sentences on the board:
1 *If I catch a fish, I'll be happy.*   **2** *If I caught 20 fish, I'd be very happy.*
Ask students to explain the difference between the two sentences.

● ***Could* and *might*** Explain to students that *could* (= *would be able to*) and *might* (= *perhaps I*, etc. *would*) are often used in 2nd conditional sentences. Write these examples:
*I **could go** to the concert if I had a ticket.*
*If you went to bed earlier, you **might feel** better.*
Then ask questions like:
What could you do if you had $1 million? (If I had $1 million, I could …)
What might happen if an asteroid hit the earth? (If an asteroid hit the earth, we might …)

Extension

● **Improbability** We can often use *were* after *I/he/she/it* in 2nd conditional sentences to emphasise the improbability of the event or situation.
*If I **were** you, I'd phone the police.*   (OR If I was you …)
*If Sarah **were** here, she'd know what to do.*   (OR If Sarah was here …)

Answers to WHAT'S THE RULE? **12:**
A 2; 1   **B** b   **C** b   **REMEMBER! 1** *present simple* **2** *past simple*

When do we use *would* in *if*-sentences?

If we had a car, the journey would be easier. If I lived near the sea, I could go to the beach every day.

● **Ist or 2nd conditional?**

Students work in pairs. They have to create two key sentences that demonstrate the difference between real possibility (1st conditional) and an improbable or imaginary situation (2nd conditional). The two sentences should be similar in content.

Examples:
If I win £10, I'll buy you a drink.
(A real possibility that he'll win £10.)

If I won £1000, I'd buy you a bottle of champagne.
(It's very unlikely he'll win £1000.)

If my team wins 1-0, I'll be happy.
(They might win 1-0. It's a possibility.)

If my team won 10-0, I'd be very, very happy.
(It's very unlikely they'll score 10 goals.)

Students then read their sentences to the class. Encourage the class to discuss any 'doubtful' sentences.

● **Why would you do that?**

Write the following actions on the board (think of others if you like):
1 *Steal money.*
2 *Take all my clothes off in public.*
3 *Tell a lie.*
4 *Jump into the sea with all my clothes on.*

Ask students: *Would you do these things? Why?* Tell them to work in groups and discuss possible reasons they might have for doing these things. Finally they decide on one or two 2nd conditional sentences for each thing.

Example:
I would steal money if my children didn't have any food.

● **Consequences**

Give the class the leading *if*-clause of a 2nd conditional sentence. Write it on the board:

Examples:
If I was/were rich ...
OR *If I could go anywhere in the world ...*

Ask one student to complete the sentence.

Example:
If I could go anywhere in the world, I'd go to Tahiti.

Ask a second student: *And what would you do if you went to Tahiti?*

Answer: *If I went to Tahiti, I'd live by the sea.*

Then get students to work in groups. One member of the group writes his/her first sentence on a sheet of paper. The sentence can include the *if*-clause that you've written on the board, or the student can think of a completely new leading sentence. Then he/she passes the sheet of paper to another member of the group who writes a following 2nd conditional sentence, and so on, until each member of the group has written a sentence.

Finally each group reads its list of sentences to the class.

Example:
If I could go anywhere in the world, I'd go to Tahiti. ▶ *If I went to Tahiti, I'd live by the sea.* ▶ *If I lived by the sea, I'd have a boat.* ▶ *If I had a boat, I'd go fishing. etc.*

Answers to PRACTICE EXERCISES 12:
1 1d 2a 3b 4c   **2** 1 would be 2 went 3 wouldn't have 4 didn't go 5 got 6 worked 7 would visit 8 would be 9 wouldn't have to 10 told   **3** 1 went 2 'd/would miss 3 didn't go 4 wouldn't have 5 did 6 weren't   **4** 1 *If I won a lot of money, I'd/would go to live in the USA.* 2 *I wouldn't need English lessons if I spoke perfect English.* 3 *My English would be better if I spent two years in England.* 4 *My life would be easier if everyone in the world learned Russian.*

PRACTICE EXERCISES 12

When do we use *would* in *if*-sentences?

If we had a car, the journey would be easier. If I lived near the sea, I could go to the beach every day.

1 Match the sentences with the explanations.

1 If Manchester United win the Championship, their fans will be happy. ☐ d

2 If I went to work in another country, it would be Japan. ☐

3 If Manchester United won the Championship, their fans would be very happy. ☐

4 If I go to work in another country, it'll be Japan. ☐

a This is an English schoolgirl who dreams of going to Japan.
b Manchester United haven't won a match so far this year.
c This is a salesman who works for an international company.
d Manchester United have won all their matches so far this year.

2 Sarah's imagining her future. <u>Underline</u> the correct verb form.

My parents (1 *were / <u>would be</u>*) very disappointed if I didn't go to university. If I (2 *would go / went*) to university, I'd have to study for three more years and I (3 *didn't have / wouldn't have*) any money. If I (4 *didn't go / wouldn't go*) to university, I could get a job. And if I (5 *would get / got*) a job, I'd have some money! If I (6 *worked / would work*) for two years, I might have enough money to travel for a year. If I went to Australia, I (7 *visit / would visit*) my uncle Harry. I'm sure he (8 *was / would be*) pleased if I went to see him. And if I was in Australia, I (9 *didn't have to / wouldn't have to*) speak a foreign language. I'm going to write to uncle Harry, but I won't tell my parents. If I (10 *tell / told*) them, they'd be angry.

3 Put the verbs into the correct form.

ANNE: Are you coming into town on Saturday?
TOM: No. If I (1 go) ......*went*...... into town, I'd spend too much money. And I don't want to go out in the afternoon. I (2 miss) .... the match on TV if I went out.
ANNE: What about Sunday morning?
TOM: I'm seeing my grandmother. She'd be very disappointed if I (3 not go) ....
ANNE: Well, what about a game of tennis on Sunday afternoon?
TOM: No. I (4 not have) .... time to do my homework if I played tennis.
ANNE: You could play if you (5 do) .... your homework in the evening.
TOM: No. I go to bed early on Sundays.
ANNE: You're so boring, Tom! If you (6 not be) .... so boring, I'd invite you to my party tonight!

4 These students are talking about improbable future events or situations. Write *if*-sentences.

1 PASCAL: win a lot of money / go to live in the USA.
If I ...*won a lot of money, I'd (would) go to live in the USA.*...

2 MIGUEL: not need English lessons / speak perfect English
I ....

3 KARIN: be better / spend two years in England
My English ....

4 IGOR: be easier / everyone in the world / learn / Russian
My life ....

DESIGNED TO PHOTOCOPY

51

When do we use *would have* in *if*-sentences?

If Sally had worked harder, she would have passed the exam.
If we had played better, we might have won the match.

A

Ed didn't hear his alarm clock yesterday morning. He didn't wake up. He didn't catch the bus.

If + PAST PERFECT   +   *would have*
If he **had heard** his alarm clock, he **would have woken up**. (NOT If he ~~would have~~ heard)

This is an example of the 3rd conditional. Answer the question.

1 Are we talking about the future, the present or the past here? ....

Now complete this sentence.

2 If he (wake up) ....…............ at the usual time, he (catch) ....…..…........... the bus.

B Ed missed the bus. He was late for school.

If + PAST PERFECT   +   *wouldn't have*
If he **hadn't missed** the bus, he **wouldn't have been** late for school.

Notice the negative forms of the verbs in this example.

Now complete this sentence.
He ate a hamburger for lunch. He was ill in the afternoon.

If he (eat) ....…............ the hamburger, he (be) ....…..…........... ill.

C Ed wanted to go to a football match yesterday evening, but he didn't buy a ticket.

If + PAST PERFECT   +   *could have*
If he **had bought** a ticket, he **could have gone** to the match.

Ed didn't have a good day yesterday. He didn't stay in bed!

If + PAST PERFECT   +   *might have*
If he **had stayed** in bed, he **might have had** a better day!

We often use *could have* (= *would have been able to*) and *might have* (= *perhaps he would have*) in 3rd conditional sentences. Complete this sentence:

If he (not go) ....…..................... to bed late, he (might + hear) ....…..................... his alarm clock.

Note that *if* can come at the beginning or in the middle of the sentence.
If he had heard his alarm clock, he would have woken up.
OR He would have woken up *if* he had heard his alarm clock.

┌─ **REMEMBER!** ───

1 **Complete this rule:**
  The 3rd conditional = If + ...…..…... + *would have*

2 **Which alternative (*a* or *b*) completes the rule?** ☐
  We use a 3rd conditional sentence to talk about …
  (**a**) things that really happened in the past. (**b**) things that didn't happen but that we imagine.

└──

🐈 *DESIGNED TO PHOTOCOPY*

When do we use *would have* in *if*-sentences?

If Sally had worked harder, she would have passed the exam.
If we had played better, we might have won the match.

The problem: Students aren't sure which tenses to use in the 3rd conditional.
Typical mistakes: *If the weather ~~would have been~~ better, I would have gone to the beach.*
If you'~~d have~~ asked me, I would have lent you the money.
If I had been there, I ~~had seen~~ him.

● **Use and form of the 3rd conditional** Describe what happened to an American girl
who was on holiday in Mexico. Say: *Hannah went to the beach. She didn't leave her bag
in the hotel. The bag wasn't safe on the beach.*
Write on the board: *If Hannah had left her bag in the hotel, it would have been safe.*
Ask students: *Am I talking about the future, the present or the past? (The past.)*
Ask: *What tense did I use after **If**? (**had left** = past perfect.)*
Ask: *Which tense did I use in the main clause? (**would have** = past conditional.)*
Write on the board: 3rd conditional = *If* + past perfect + *would have*

● **Using the 3rd conditional** Continue the story:
Someone stole Hannah's bag. Her return ticket to New York was in the bag.
Without her ticket, she missed the plane. She also missed a job interview the next day.
Write key words on the board: *return ticket/miss the plane/job interview*
Now write these half sentences: **1** *If she hadn't taken her bag to the beach, the thief ...*
                                 2 *If her return ticket hadn't been in her bag, she ...*
                                 3 *If she had caught her plane, she ...*
Ask one student to come to the board and complete Sentence 1 *(wouldn't have stolen her bag).*
Encourage other students to help. Ask different students to do the same with 2 and 3.

● **More practice** Finish telling the story:
She didn't leave Mexico that day. The next day she met Luis, a Mexican man.
She didn't go back to the USA. She married Luis!
Write key words on the board: *didn't leave Mexico/ Luis didn't go back/ married Luis*
Get students to think of two more sentences in the 3rd conditional.
Examples: *If she had left Mexico that day, she wouldn't have met Luis.*
          She would have gone back to the USA if she hadn't married Luis.

● ***Could have*** and ***might have*** Say to the class:
*There wasn't another plane to New York that day so she **couldn't go** to the interview.*
Ask students to make a 3rd conditional sentence:
*If there **had been** another plane to New York, she **could have gone** to the interview.*
Then say: *She didn't go to the interview. **Perhaps** she would have got the job.*
Ask students to make another 3rd conditional sentence:
*If she **had gone** to the interview, she **might have got** the job.*
Tell students that we often use *could have* and *might have* in 3rd conditional sentences:
could have = would have been able to
might have = perhaps they would have

Answers to WHAT'S THE RULE? 13:
A 1 *The past.* **2** *had woken up; would have caught*   **B** *hadn't eaten; wouldn't have been*   **C** *hadn't gone; might have heard*
REMEMBER! 1 *past perfect/had ...* **2** b

When do we use *would have* in *if*-sentences?

If Sally had worked harder, she would have passed the exam.
If we had played better, we might have won the match.

- **Regrets**

  Students think of three things they have done or not done in the past.

  Examples:
  I didn't work very hard last year.
  I went to bed very late last night.
  I met my girlfriend/boyfriend in hospital.

  They then write sentences in which they explain what happened as a result of what they did or didn't do.

  Examples:
  If I'd worked harder, I would have passed the exam.
  If I hadn't gone to bed late, I wouldn't have felt so tired next morning.
  If I hadn't broken my leg, I wouldn't have met my girlfriend/boyfriend.

  Students work in groups. They compare and discuss their sentences and read out the most interesting ones to the rest of the class.

- **Consequences**

  Say: *The weather was terrible last Saturday.*

  Write this *if*-clause on the board: *If the weather had been better ...*

  Ask a student: *What would you have done if the weather had been better?*

  Example answer:
  If the weather had been better, I would have gone into town.

  Ask another student: *What would you have done if you'd gone into town?*

  Example answer:
  If I'd gone into town, I would have bought some new jeans.

Now get students to work in groups. Student A writes an *if*-clause (*If + had*). He/she passes it to Student B who completes the sentence. Student C then writes another *if*-clause and passes it on to Student D to complete, and so on.

- **Events that changed history**

  Students work in groups and think of historical events that changed history.

  Examples:
  Bell invented the telephone.
  Columbus 'discovered' America.
  Mr and Mrs Presley had a son called Elvis.
  Nelson Mandela became President of South Africa.
  Logie Baird invented television.

  Each group thinks of sentences, using the 3rd conditional, in which they speculate about what might have happened if ...

  Examples:
  If Bell hadn't invented the telephone...,
  I wouldn't have spent an hour on the phone last night. OR *I couldn't have talked to my brother in California.*

Answers to PRACTICE EXERCISES 13:
1 1 a *False.* b *True.* 2 a *False.* b *True.* **2** 1 *If I hadn't been shy, I would have had more friends.* 2 *If I'd/had been clever, I would have done well at school.* 3 *My mother wouldn't have got a job if my father hadn't died.* 4 *If my mother hadn't been ill, she wouldn't have lost her job.* 5 *I would have had a boyfriend if I'd been pretty.* **3** 1 *wouldn't have been* 2 *'d/had given* 3 *had been* 4 *could have talked* 5 *'d/had let* 6 *could have phoned* 7 *'d/had asked* 8 *would have helped* 9 *'d/had been* 10 *might have enjoyed* **4** 1 *If you'd/had asked me, I would have danced with you.* 2 *I would have said goodbye if you'd wanted to speak to me.* 3 *If I'd had your phone number, I would have phoned you.* 4 *I wouldn't have gone out with another girl if you hadn't gone out with another boy!*

When do we use *would have* in *if*-sentences?

If Sally had worked harder, she would have passed the exam.
If we had played better, we might have won the match.

1 Read these sentences. Write *True* or *False* after the explanations.

   1 If we'd hurried, we would have caught the train.

   a They hurried. ...*False*..............   **b** They didn't catch the train. ....…..

   2 We wouldn't have missed the train if it had been 5 minutes late.

   a The train was 5 minutes late. ....…...   **b** They missed the train. ....…..

2 An old woman is talking about her life. Rewrite the sentences.

   1 I was shy. I didn't have many friends. If ...*I hadn't been shy, I would have had more friends.*.........

   2 I didn't do well at school because I wasn't very clever.

   If .... , ...

   3 My father died when I was young. My mother got a job.

   .... if ....

   4 My mother lost her job. She was ill.

   If .... ill, ...

   5 I never had a boyfriend. I wasn't pretty.

   I .... if ....

3 Jaime studied English at a language school last summer. He stayed with an English woman, Diana. But there were problems. Put the verbs into the correct form.

   JAIME: I was always hungry. I (1 not be) ...*wouldn't have been*.... so hungry if she (2 give) .... me more food.

   DIANA: I couldn't talk to him. If his English (3 be) .... better, I (4 could/talk) .... to him more.

   JAIME: She never let me use the phone. If she (5 let) .... me use the phone,

          I (6 could/phone) .... my parents.

   DIANA: He never asked me to help him. If he (7 ask) .... me,

          I (8 help) .... him with his homework

   JAIME: I didn't enjoy my stay. If she (9 be) .... more friendly,

          I (10 might/enjoy) .... my stay.

4 Tom and Jenny have had an argument at a party. Write Tom's second sentence.

   JENNY: You didn't dance with me.

   TOM: You didn't ask me. (1) If ....*you'd (had) asked me, I would have danced with you.*..........

   JENNY: You didn't say goodbye.

   TOM: You didn't want to speak to me. (2) I .... goodbye

          if ....

   JENNY: You didn't phone me.

   TOM: I didn't have your phone number. (3) If I .... ,

          ....

   JENNY: You went out with another girl.

   TOM: You went out with another boy! (4) I ....

          if ....!

I wish + past simple OR + past perfect OR + *would/could*?

I wish I knew the answer. I wish I had bought a bigger car. I wish she would write to me. I wish I could swim.

A *wish* + PAST SIMPLE
Kate and Mark are walking home after a concert.
It's late, it's dark, and they haven't got a car.

KATE: I wish I **was** at home in bed.
    (NOT I wish I ~~would be~~ at home ...)
    I wish it **wasn't** so dark.
    (NOT I wish it ~~wouldn't be~~ so dark.)
    I wish we **had** a car.
    (NOT I wish we ~~would have~~ a car.)

They haven't got an umbrella.

Complete what Mark says.

MARK: I wish we ………..……. an umbrella.

B *wish* + PAST PERFECT
The concert didn't finish on time, so they missed the last bus.

MARK: I wish the concert **had finished** on time.
    I wish we **hadn't missed** the last bus.

They left at the end of the concert.

Complete what Kate says.

KATE: I wish we ………………… before the end.

C *wish* + *would*
Mark wants a car to stop. But the cars are going
too fast. Mark and Kate are both very wet!

MARK: I wish someone **would stop** for us.
    (NOT I wish someone ~~stopped~~ for us.)
    I wish they **wouldn't go** so fast.
    (NOT I wish they ~~didn't~~ go so fast.)

It's still raining.

Complete what Mark says.

MARK: I wish it ………………… stop raining.

D *I / We wish* + *I / we could*
Mark hasn't got a car, because he can't drive.

MARK: I wish I **could drive**.   (NOT I wish I ~~would~~ drive.)

They can't find a taxi.

Complete what Kate says.

KATE: I wish we ………………… find a taxi.

REMEMBER!

Complete these rules. Write *would*, the PS (past simple) or the PP (past perfect).

1 We use ………………..……. after *I wish* when we imagine a present situation being different.

2 We use ………………..……. after *I wish* when we regret something that happened or didn't happen in the past.

3 We use ………………..……. after *I wish* when we want something to happen or someone else to do something.

4 We use *would* when we want <u>someone else</u> to do something. So we can't say *I wish **I** would*
    or ***We* wish *we* would**. (*I wish **a car** would stop.* BUT *I wish **I** could phone my dad.*)

      **DESIGNED TO PHOTOCOPY**

I wish + past simple OR + past perfect OR + would/could?

I wish I knew the answer. I wish I had bought a bigger car. I wish she would write to me. I wish I could swim.

The problem: Students often confuse the use of *would* and the past simple or past perfect after *I wish*. And they mistakenly use *would* after *I wish I …* and *I wish we …* .

Typical mistakes:
I wish someone ~~helped~~ me.	(I wish someone would help me.)
I wish I ~~would be~~ on holiday.	(I wish I was on holiday.)
I wish I ~~would buy~~ a car.	(I wish I could buy a car.)
I wish I ~~would have seen~~ the match.	(I wish I had seen the match.)

● **Differences between the constructions used after *I wish*** Write these sentences on the board:

JACK: **1** *I'm not good-looking.*   **2** *I bought this sweater yesterday, but I don't like it.*
   3 *I want Kate to invite me to her party.*   **4** *I want to find a girlfriend.*

Indicate Sentence 1. Say: *Jack wants to be good-looking. So what does he say?*
   (I wish I was good-looking.)

Indicate Sentence 2. Say: *He bought the sweater, but he regrets it. What does he say?*
   (I wish I hadn't bought it.)

Indicate Sentence 3. Say: *He wants Kate to do something. What does he say?*
   (I wish Kate would invite me to her party.)

Indicate Sentence 4. Say: *He wants to do something. What does he say?*
   (I wish I could find a girlfriend.)

Then discuss with students the basic rules governing *wish*:

wish + the past simple = We imagine the present situation being different.

wish + the past perfect = We regret a past action or situation.

wish + *would* = We want something to happen, or somebody else to do something.

I/we wish + *could* = We do not use *would* after *I/we wish*.

● **Check students' understanding** Do some rapid oral work. Give the class prompts, and tell them to make sentences with *I wish*.
Examples:

I'm not rich.	▶ *I wish I **was** rich.*
I don't live in a nice flat.	▶ *I wish I **lived** in a nice flat.*
I live next to a prison.	▶ *I wish I **didn't live** next to a prison.*
I haven't got a job.	▶ *I wish I **had** a job.*
I want someone to give me a job.	▶ *I wish someone **would give** me a job.*
I want to stop smoking.	▶ *I wish I **could stop** smoking.*
I didn't pass my exams.	▶ *I wish I'**d/had passed** my exams.*

● **The short form '*d* = *had* or *would*** Remind students of the meaning of *'d*.

I wish you'd phoned me.	▶ *I wish you **had phoned** me.*
I wish you'd close the window.	▶ *I wish you **would close** the window.*

Extension

● **Use of *were*** In *wish*-sentences we sometimes use *were*, instead of *was*, after *I/he/she/it*. This emphasises the 'impossibility' of the wish. *I wish I **were** older.* OR *I wish I **was** older.*

Answers to WHAT'S THE RULE? 14:
A *had*   **B** *'d/had left*   **C** *would*   **D** *could*   **REMEMBER! 1** *the past simple* **2** *the past perfect* **3** *would*

14 CLASSROOM ACTIVITIES

I wish + past simple OR + past perfect OR + *would/could*?

I wish I knew the answer. I wish I had bought a bigger car. I wish she would write to me. I wish I could swim.

● **What do you wish?**

Write the following on the board:

1 *What do you want to change about your life at the moment (your present situation)?*
2 *What past actions do you regret?*
3 *What would you like someone to do?*
4 *What would you like to happen?*
5 *What things can't you do, which you'd like to do?*

Students work in pairs and tell each other their wishes.

They then write their own sentences, beginning *I wish … .*

Students can then read out their most interesting wishes to the rest of the class.

Examples:

1 *I wish I was two years older. I wish I didn't have a long nose.*
2 *I wish my parents had given me a different name.*
3 *I wish people would stop destroying the earth.*
4 *I wish my sister wouldn't read my letters.*
5 *I wish I could play the guitar.*

● **Guess who it is**

Tell students to think of another student in the class. They then make a sentence which they think the other student would say, beginning *I wish... .*

They then ask the class *Who would say this?* and read out their sentence.

The rest of the class try to identify the student in question.

Examples:

Who would say this? I wish I had a Ducati 9000.
(*Dimitri* – The class knows that Dimitri is mad about motorbikes.)

Who would say this? I wish Camillo would go out with me.
(*Sophia* – The class knows that Sophia likes Camillo.)

● **What are they thinking?**

Describe a situation and ask the class what the person in question might be thinking.

Say to the class: *A woman is looking in a shop window. She's looking at a black dress. What's she thinking? Begin with 'I wish'.*

Students make suggestions:
I wish I could buy that dress.
I wish I had enough money to buy that dress.
I wish that dress was mine.
I wish someone would buy that dress for me.

Other possible situations (if you like, add your own):

A man is looking at all the old drinks cans and bits of paper in the street.

A girl is at a concert watching her favourite singer.

A boy is waiting for his girlfriend outside the cinema. She's late.

Answers to PRACTICE EXERCISES 14:
1 1d 2c 3a 4b   **2** 1 <u>was</u> 2 <u>would stop</u> 3 <u>would change</u> 4 <u>lived</u> 5 <u>could go</u> 6 <u>had gone</u> 7 <u>wasn't</u> 8 <u>didn't cost</u>
3 1 *I wish I knew her phone number.* 2 *I wish I could remember her address.* 3 *I wish she didn't live 25 kilometres away.*
4 *I wish she'd/would phone me.* 5 *I wish I'd/had given her my phone number.* 6 *I wish I could see her again.*
4 1 *could speak English; could speak Spanish.* 2 *was; had long blond* 3 *'d/would* 4 *wouldn't* 5 *hadn't come*

I wish + past simple OR + past perfect OR + *would/could*?

I wish I knew the answer. I wish I had bought a bigger car. I wish she would write to me. I wish I could swim.

1 **Match the sentences with the rules.**

1 I wish we could go to the cinema tonight.   [d]

2 I wish my parents would lend me some money.   ☐

3 I wish my parents weren't so strict.   ☐

4 I wish I hadn't spent all my money.   ☐

a We use this tense after *I wish* when we imagine the present situation being different.

b We use this tense after *I wish* when we regret something that happened or didn't happen in the past.

c We use this tense after *I wish* when we want someone to do something or something to happen.

d We don't use *would* after *I wish I / We wish we … .*

2 <u>Underline</u> **the correct verb form.**

1 I wish the weather (*would be* / <u>*was*</u>) better.

2 I wish it (*stopped* / *would stop*) raining.

3 I wish the English climate (*changed* / *would change*).

4 I wish I (*lived* / *would live*) in a hot country.

5 I wish I (*would go* / *could go*) and live in Australia.

6 My brother went to live in Australia. I wish I (*would have gone* / *had gone*) with him.

7 I wish Australia (*wasn't* / *wouldn't be*) so far away.

8 I wish it (*wouldn't cost* / *didn't cost*) so much to get there.

3 **Liam met a girl at a party. He wants to see her again, but there are problems.**
Write what he says, using *I wish*.

1 He doesn't know her phone number.   *I wish I knew her phone number.* ....

2 He can't remember her address.   ....

3 She lives 25 kilometres away.   ....

4 He wants her to phone him.   ....

5 He didn't give her his phone number.   ....

6 He wants to see her again.   ....

4 **Complete Gemma's sentences.**

1 Gemma's a student. She likes Rafael, but she can't speak Spanish and he can't speak English.

GEMMA: I wish Rafael ....*could speak English.* .... I wish I ....

2 Rafael likes Sally. Sally's a model. Gemma hasn't got long blond hair like Sally.

GEMMA: I wish I .... a model. I wish I .... hair.

3 Gemma's at a club with some friends. She wants Rafael to dance with her.

GEMMA: I wish he .... dance with me.

4 Rafael's dancing with Sally. Gemma doesn't like this.

GEMMA: I wish he .... dance with Sally all the time.

5 Gemma wants to go home. She regrets coming to the club tonight.

GEMMA: I wish I .... to the club tonight.

Can OR *may/might*? *Must* OR *have to*?

I can swim. It might rain tomorrow. It's late – I must go. I have to go to the dentist's next Monday.
You mustn't smoke. You don't have to pay.

A George is a clever man. He knows how to do a lot of things.
He *can play* the piano. He *can speak* five languages.
But *can* he *cook*? No, he *can't*.
He *can't boil* an egg or *make* an omelette!

He knows how to write a poem, but he doesn't know how to use a computer.
Complete the sentence.

He .... write a poem, but he .... use a computer.

B George wants Julia to come to dinner next week.
What does she say? What are the possibilities?
I *can't see* you on Monday or Friday.
I *might* (OR *may*) *be* in London on Tuesday.   (NOT I ~~can~~ be)
I *may* (OR *might*) *not be* free on Wednesday.   (NOT I ~~can't~~ be)
I *can come* on Thursday.

Complete the sentences.

1 Julia's free on Thursday. She .... have dinner with George on Thursday.

2 It's possible she'll be at home on Wednesday. She .... be at home on Wednesday.

3 It isn't possible for her to come on Monday. She .... come on Monday.

4 It's possible she won't be at home on Tuesday. She .... be at home on Tuesday.

C There's a meeting on Monday. It's necessary for Julia to go.
JULIA: I *have to go* to a meeting on Monday.   (Other people want Julia to go to the meeting.)
     I *must check* the time of the meeting.   (Julia wants to check the time of the meeting.)
Complete these sentences, using *have to* and *must*.

I .... go to a conference on Friday. I .... buy a new jacket.

D Julia's friend Anne is having a party on Wednesday.
Anne says to her: You *don't have to come* to my party.   (= You can come if you like, but it isn't necessary.)
She doesn't say: You *mustn't come* to my party.   (= Don't come to my party!)
Complete these sentences, using *mustn't* or *don't have to*.

The party starts at 8.00. I .... be late. I can take a taxi, so I .... take my car.

REMEMBER!

Complete the sentences, using *can, can't, may (not)/might (not)*:

1 I .... play the piano.   (I know how to play the piano.)

2 I .... come tomorrow.   (It's possible for me to come tomorrow.)

3 I .... come tomorrow.   (Perhaps I'll come tomorrow. I'm not sure.)

4 I .... come tomorrow.   (It's impossible for me to come tomorrow.)

5 I .... come tomorrow.   (Perhaps I won't come tomorrow. I'm not sure.)

Now complete these sentences, using *must/mustn't, have to/don't have to*:

6 I can't come tomorrow morning. I .... see my manager at 10.00.
(The obligation comes from the manager, not from the speaker.)

7 There's a mistake in this report. I .... tell my manager.
(This is the speaker's personal intention/opinion. The obligation comes from the speaker.)

8 You .... take the car to London. I need it. (Don't take the car!)

9 You .... take the car to London. You can go by train. (It isn't necessary to take the car.)

Can OR *may/might? Must* OR *have to?*

I can swim. It might rain tomorrow. It's late – I must go. I have to go to the dentist's next Monday.
You mustn't smoke. You don't have to pay.

The problem:	For possibility, students often confuse *can* and *may/might.*
	I can come tomorrow. = It's possible for me to come tomorrow.
	I may come tomorrow. = Perhaps I'll come tomorrow. I'm not sure. (NOT can)
	For obligation, we can sometimes use either *must* or *have to,* but in certain contexts they have a different meaning. Students often don't understand this difference.
	Must = <u>the speaker</u> has made the decision. He imposes the obligation on himself.
	Have to = <u>somebody else</u> has made the decision. The obligation is from outside the speaker.
	Students also need to be clear about the difference between *mustn't* and *don't have to.*
Typical mistakes:	*He can ~~to~~ come. He ~~cans~~ come.* ~~*Does he can*~~ *come?*
	Don't phone him – he ~~can~~ be ill. *It ~~can~~ rain tomorrow.*
	He ~~must~~ wash his clothes – his mother doesn't wash them for him.
	You ~~don't have to~~ smoke. It's bad for you.

● **Can for ability/possibility** Write these two sentences on the board:
I can play the guitar. I can come to your party tomorrow.

Tell students that *can* is used for ability and possibility. If, in their language, students would use one verb for ability and another for possibility, translate the two English sentences to show the dual use of *can.* (NB *Can* is used also for permission.)

● **Possibilities** Demonstrate the difference in meaning between *can* and *may/might.*
Tell the class that you're planning to go to X (choose a suitable destination).

Then write this sentence on the board: **1** *I can go to X by train or by bus.*
Ask the class: *What are the two general possibilities? (You can go by train or by bus.)*

Tell the class that you aren't sure what you're going to do. Write: **2** *I might go by train.*
Ask the class: *Is it possible to go by train?*, and indicate sentence 1. *(Yes.)*

Then ask: *Will I go by train? Am I sure that I will go by train? (You aren't sure. You might go by train.)*

● **Obligation** Write these sentences on the board:
1 *I've got terrible toothache. I must go to the dentist's.*
2 *Sally's feeling nervous! She has to go to the dentist's at 10.00.*

Get students to try to explain the difference between the two sentences on the board.
Then check students' understanding of the negative forms *mustn't* and *don't have to.*

Write these two notices on the board:
SILENCE!   *FREE CONCERT TONIGHT!*

Ask them to make a sentence, using either *mustn't* or *don't have to,* after each notice.
Silence! ▶ *You mustn't talk.*   Free concert tonight! ▶ *You don't have to pay.*

Extension

● ***Have got to*** We often use *have got to* instead of *have to* when we're talking about a specific situation rather than an habitual one. *He's very ill. He's got to have an operation tomorrow.*

Answers to WHAT'S THE RULE? **15:**
A *can; can't*   **B** 1 *can* 2 *may/might* 3 *can't* 4 *may not/might not*   **C** *have to; must*   **D** *mustn't; don't have to*
REMEMBER! 1 *can* 2 *can* 3 *may/might* 4 *can't* 5 *may not/might not* 6 *have to* 7 *must* 8 *mustn't* 9 *don't have to*

Can OR *may/might? Must* OR *have to?*

I can swim. It might rain tomorrow. It's late – I must go. I have to go to the dentist's next Monday.
You mustn't smoke. You don't have to pay.

● **What are you good at?**

Students practise the use of *can* for ability.

Students work in pairs, A and B. They ask each other questions, until they find:

1 three things which A can do, but B can't.
2 three things that A can't do, but B can.
3 three things they can both do.

Students then tell the rest of the class what they've found out about each other.

Examples:
1 *I can ski, but Marco can't.*
2 *Marco can ride a horse, but I can't.*
3 *We can both play chess.*

● **Where's my pen?**

Get students to practise the use of *may* and *might.*

Mime having lost your pen.
Say to the class: *I can't find my pen. Where do you think it might be?*

Students shout out possibilities.

Examples:
It might be in your bag.
It may be under those books.

If you hear a suggestion with *can*, explain again that we don't use *can* in these sentences where we're talking about uncertainty.

● **Things you must do**

Students practise the use of *must* for obligations that are personal opinions.

Explain to the class a problem that you have. They then tell you what you must do.
Teacher: *I always feel tired.*
Students: *You must go to bed earlier. You must see a doctor. You must stop teaching.*

Then ask students to explain their problems and ask the class to give their opinion and to say what they think is necessary.

● **What do you have to do?**

Write these places and situations on the board:
On a plane.
In an English class.
In a luxury hotel.
In a church.
In a restaurant.

Then write these verbs:
you mustn't
you don't have to
you have to

Get students to work in pairs. Give each pair one of the places/situations. Students write at least three sentences, using each of the verbs on the board.

They then read out their sentences to the rest of the class.

Examples:
On a plane, you mustn't smoke in the toilets.
You have to sit down when the plane is landing.
You don't have to eat the food that they give you.

Answers to PRACTICE EXERCISES 15:
1 1e 2d 3c 4a 5b **2** 1 *Can* 2 *can't* 3 *can* 4 *might/may* 5 *can't* 6 *may/might* 7 *might/may* 8 *may/might*
9 *may not/might not* **3** 1 *don't have to* 2 *mustn't* 3 *don't have to* 4 *mustn't* **4** 1 *must* 2 *have to* 3 *has to* 4 *have to*
5 *have to* 6 *mustn't* 7 *don't have to* 8 *must*

Can OR *may/might?* Must OR *have to?*

I can swim. It might rain tomorrow. It's late – I must go. I have to go to the dentist's next Monday. You mustn't smoke. You don't have to pay.

1 Match the sentences with the correct explanations.

1 I can go to the club on Saturday. I'm free.   `e`   a It isn't possible.

2 But I don't think I'll go, because I can't dance.   ☐   b It's possible, but it isn't certain.

3 All my friends can dance, so I feel stupid.   ☐   c They know how to do it.

4 Kelly's broken her leg, so she can't dance.   ☐   d I don't know how to do it.

5 But she might go to the club to meet her friends.   ☐   e It's possible for me to go.

2 Complete this conversation, using *can/can't* or *may (not)/might (not)*.

HELEN: (1) .....*Can*...... you hear that noise? What is it?

JAMES: What noise? I (2) .... hear anything.

HELEN: I'm sure I (3) .... hear a noise outside.

JAMES: It (4) .... be the wind.

HELEN: It (5) .... be the wind. It isn't windy tonight.

JAMES: It (6) .... be a cat.

HELEN: A cat? Well, it isn't our cat. He's upstairs.

JAMES: It (7) .... be the neighbour's cat.

HELEN: Go outside and see what it is.

JAMES: I'm not going out! It (8) .... be a man with a gun.

      You (9) .... see me again!

3 What do these notices mean? Complete the sentences, using *mustn't* or *don't have to*.

1 FREE PARKING — You .....*don't have to*..... to pay to park your car.

2 NO DOGS ON THE BEACH — You .... take your dog on the beach.

3 NON-MEMBERS WELCOME — You can go into the club. You .... to be a member.

4 DANGER! KEEP OUT! — You .... go through this door.

4 Complete the sentences, using *must, have to/has to, mustn't* or *don't have to*.

SAM: There's a brilliant film at the Odeon. We (1) .....*must*...... see it. Can anyone come with me tonight?

SARAH: No, I can't come. I (2) .... look after my little brother tonight, because my mother won't be at home. She (3) .... go to a meeting.

TOM: I'm afraid I can't come. I (4) .... stay in on Fridays. My parents don't let me go out. I (5) .... to do my homework.

SAM: But it's a great film. You (6) .... miss it.

TOM: I can't come, Sam. It's OK for you. You (7) .... work tonight, but I've got no choice. Perhaps Laura can come.

SAM: That's a good idea. I (8) .... phone her.

Published by

DELTA Publishing
Quince Cottage
Hoe Lane
Surrey GU5 9SW
England

© David Bolton and
Noel Goodey 1999

First published 1999
Reprinted 2001, 2006, 2009

ISBN 0 953 3098 4 3
ISBN 978 0 953309 84 9

Edited by Sally McGugan

Illustrations by John Plumb

Designed by Christine Cox

Printed by Halstan & Co. Ltd.,
Amersham, Buckinghamshire,
England

DELTA PUBLISHING aims to provide teachers of English –
wherever they are and whatever their teaching
situation – with innovative, creative, practical
resource materials to help them in their everyday
teaching tasks.

For further information and a copy of the latest
DELTA PUBLISHING catalogue, please contact:

DELTA Publishing
Quince Cottage
Hoe Lane
Surrey GU5 9SW
England

Email info@deltapublishing.co.uk
Web www.deltapublishing.co.uk

Creative materials for creative teachers

Also by David Bolton and Noel Goodey

**TROUBLE WITH ADJECTIVES, ADVERBS
AND PRONOUNS?**
ISBN 0 953 3098 7 8
ISBN 978 0 953309 87 0

**TROUBLE WITH PREPOSITIONS, ARTICLES,
NOUNS AND WORD ORDER?**
ISBN 0 953 3098 5 1
ISBN 978 0 953309 86 6